Alan Power Exposed
Hundreds of Errors in
"The Princess Diana Conspiracy"

Book Review of *The Princess Diana Conspiracy: The Evidence of Murder* by Alan Power, 2013, published by Probity Press Ltd, Hardcover Edition

John Morgan is author of *Paris-London Connection: The Assassination of Princess Diana* and also the *Diana Inquest* series

Website: www.princessdianadeaththeevidence.weebly.com

© John Morgan 2013

First published in Australia by Shining Bright Publishing

This edition printed in USA

ISBN: 978-1494318192

"The volumes written by John Morgan will come to be regarded as the 'Magnum Opus' on the crash"
> – Michael Mansfield, QC, who served at the 2007-8 inquest

"John Morgan has done more to expose the facts of this case than the police in France and Britain"
> – Mohamed Al Fayed, who lost his son Dodi in the crash

"John Morgan is indisputably the world's leading expert on the assassination of Princess Diana"
> – *Uncensored* magazine

Books by John Morgan

Paris-London Connection: The Assassination of Princess Diana (2012)
A short, easy-to read, fast-moving synopsis of the complete story of the events, including the lead-up, the crash and the ensuing cover-up – based on the *Diana Inquest* series

Cover-Up of a Royal Murder: Hundreds of Errors in the Paget Report (2007)
Exposes major flaws in the report by the official **British** police investigation into the Paris crash

The *Diana Inquest* Series

Part 1: Diana Inquest: **The Untold Story** (2009)
Covers pre-crash events in the Ritz Hotel, the final journey and what happened in the Alma Tunnel

Part 2: Diana Inquest: **How & Why Did Diana Die?** (2009)
Covers possible motives for assassination and post-crash medical treatment of Princess Diana – including mistreatment in the ambulance

Part 3: Diana Inquest: **The French Cover-Up** (2010)
Covers the autopsies of the driver, Henri Paul, and the misconduct of the French investigation into the crash

Part 4: Diana Inquest: **The British Cover-Up** (2011)
Covers the post-death treatment of Princess Diana – including the embalmings and autopsies carried out in both France and the UK and the post-crash cover-up by UK authorities, including the Queen

Part 5: Diana Inquest: **Who Killed Princess Diana?** (2012)
Covers the involvement of MI6 and senior British royals in the assassinations of Princess Diana and Dodi Fayed

Part 6: Diana Inquest: **Corruption at Scotland Yard** (2013)
Exposes one of the biggest cover-ups in Scotland Yard history – it
uncovers police corruption on a scale that should shock most members
of the British public

Diana Inquest: **The Documents the Jury Never Saw** (2010)
Reproduces hundreds of key documents from within the British Paget
investigation – all documents that the inquest jury were prevented from
seeing

Contents

Acknowledgements 15

Introduction 17

Why This Review? 19

The Errors 21

Pre-1997 23

    1.   *Diana and Charles' divorce* 23

    2.   *Queen's order for divorce – Timing* 25

    3.   *Loss of HRH title announcement – Timing* 25

    4.   *Panorama interview - Timing* 26

    5.   *Diana's engagement ring* 26

    6.   *Lucia-Diana recording* 27

Build-Up to Paris 29

    7.   *Threat from Nicholas Soames* 29

    8.   *Swan Lake performance – Venue* 30

    9.   *Dodi's Paris to St Tropez trip – Timing* 30

    10.   *Diana's announcement* 30

    11.   *St Tropez holiday – Diana and Dodi* 31

    12.   *Diana and Dodi's relationship – Timing* 31

    13.   *"Kiss" Photo – Timing* 31

    14.   *Engagement ring order – Timing and circumstances* ...32

    15.   *Malibu property – Omission* 32

    16.   *Richard Spearman's arrival in Paris – Timing* 33

MI6 35

    17.   *Rogue elements in MI6 – Dearlove* 35

    18.   *Assassination handouts – Miss X* 35

    19.   *The Order Book – Mr E* 37

    20.   *Interviewing of Mr A – Dearlove* 37

    21.   *Ephemeral and deniability* 38

    22.   *Dearlove in Paris* 39

    23.   *MI6 at British Embassy* 39

    24.   *MI6 in Paris – Officer evidence* 40

    25.   *Richard Spearman – Inquest identity* 40

ALAN POWER EXPOSED

26. *David Spedding – Death* *41*
27. *Robin Cook – Death* *41*

The Royals **43**

28. *Royals and the Law* *43*
29. *Way Ahead Group – Chair* *43*

Henri Paul **45**

30. *Henri Paul's General Duties - Driving* *45*
31. *Grande Remise Licence* *45*
32. *Henri Paul's Contacts List* *47*
33. *Henri Paul's bank accounts* *47*
34. *Aotal – Location* *47*
35. *Aotal packet* *48*
36. *Aotal use* *48*

Saturday, 30 August 1997 .... **49**

37. *Paparazzi pursuit – Villa Windsor* *49*
38. *Engagement ring purchase – Timing* *49*
39. *Henri Paul's movements between 7 and 10 p.m. – Alcohol* *50*
40. *Henri Paul's movements between 7 and 10 p.m. – Home visit* *51*
41. *Chez Benoît restaurant* *51*
42. *Meeting between Rees-Jones, Wingfield and Henri Paul – Location* *52*
43. *Henri Paul's condition – Willaumez-L'Hotellier* *52*
44. *Henri Paul's role – Chauffeur* *53*
45. *Decoy Mercedes* *53*
46. *Diversionary manoeuvre – Darmon* *54*
47. *Late Movements of Kez Wingfield* *54*
48. *James Andanson's movements – Ritz Hotel* *55*

The Final Journey **57**

49. *Route taken – Expressway* *57*
50. *Place de la Concorde* *58*
51. *Alexandre III Tunnel* *58*
52. *Exit before Alma Tunnel* *60*
53. *Alain Remy – Flawed Witness* *62*
54. *Alain Remy – Location* *63*

CONTENTS

55. *Pursuing motorbikes – Location* 65
56. *Pursuing motorbikes: Number – Partouche*.................................66
57. *Pursuing motorbikes: Number – Anderson*................................69
58. *Pursuing motorbikes: Number – Levistre* 70
59. *Pursuing Motorbikes: Number – Hackett* 71
60. *Pursuing Motorbikes: Number – Other witnesses* 71
61. *Mercedes' speed – Remy* 72
62. *Darmon's speed* 73

Loitering Vehicles 75

63. *"Loitering" vehicles* 75
64. *David Laurent & Blanchard family*...75
65. *David Laurent* 77
66. *Slip road* 77
67. *Gooroovadoo* 78
68. *Number*..79

In the Alma Tunnel 81

69. *Collision with wall before the Fiat Uno*...................................81
70. *White Fiat Uno – Two impacts*...81
71. *White Fiat Uno – Levistre* 82
72. *White Fiat Uno – Medjahdi*..83
73. *Mercedes' movement after Uno collision* 84
74. *Cars witnessed – Boura*..84
75. *Horn – David Laurent & Blanchard family* 85
76. *Bright flash – Witnesses* 86
77. *Bright flash – Benoît Boura & Gaëlle L'Hostis*...........................87
78. *Bright flash – Brenda Wells* 89
79. *Bright flash – Gooroovadoo & Partouche*.................................90
80. *Bright flash – Erik Petel*..92
81. *Bright Flash – Levistre timing* 92
82. *Jean Peyret – Speed* 92
83. *Jean Peyret – Position*..93
84. *Sounds heard – Jean Peyret* 93
85. *Mercedes' speed – Medjahdi* 93
86. *13th pillar*..94

ALAN POWER EXPOSED

87. Motorcyclist's gesture 94
88. Mercedes' condition post-crash 96
89. Diana's condition post-crash 97

Fleeing Vehicles 99

90. Fiat Uno post-crash – Souad 99
91. Vehicles – Lilian Blanchard 99
92. Vehicles – David Laurent & Blanchard family 100
93. Motorbike – Peyrets 101
94. Motorbike – Boura & L'Hostis 101
95. Motorbike – Grigori Rassinier 102
96. Motorbike – Jean Peyret 103
97. Vehicles – Jean Peyret & Benoît Boura 104
98. Gary Hunter – Timing 104

Ambulance & Hospital 107

99. Ambulance treatment – Omission 107
100. Ambulance stoppage en route 107
101. Hospital Events – Timing 109
102. Dr Dion's affidavit 109
103. Locating Dr Dion 110
104. Jocelyn Magellan – Male nurse 111

French Autopsies & Embalming 115

105. Henri Paul autopsies – Witness evidence 115
106. Henri Paul autopsy – Second body 115
107. Henri Paul autopsy – Number mix-up 116
108. Second autopsy – Omission 117
109. Henri Paul BAC result – Announcement 117
110. Autopsy results – Baker 120
111. Henri Paul DNA tests 121
112. Diana post-mortem – In France 122
113. Diana – Embalmer 122

James Andanson 123

114. Vierzon – Distance from Paris 123
115. Elisabeth Andanson's Paris trip 123

CONTENTS

116.	*James Andanson – Corsica trip*	*123*
117.	*Corsica trip – Timing*	*126*
118.	*Corsica trip – Photos*	*126*
119.	*James Andanson – Agency change*	*126*
120.	*Agency change – Timing*	*127*
121.	*Andanson Fiat Uno Sale - Timing*	*127*
122.	*Andanson Fiat Uno Condition*	*128*
123.	*Andanson-Dards discussion – Timing*	*128*
124.	*Death – Distance from home*	*129*
125.	*Death – Timing*	*129*
126.	*James Jnr's car racing costs*	*129*
127.	*Philippe Poincloux*	*131*
128.	*Inquest handling of Andanson*	*131*

Mishcon Note **133**

129.	*Author*	*133*
130.	*Content*	*135*
131.	*Time suppressed*	*135*
132.	*MPS-Mishcon discussions*	*135*
133.	*Timing of disclosure*	*136*
134.	*Disclosure to media*	*136*
135.	*Timing of post-Burrell Note contact*	*137*
136.	*Lord Mishcon death – Timing & cause*	*137*
137.	*Burrell Note – Timing of disclosure*	*138*

Police Investigations **139**

138.	*French Investigation - Duration*	*139*
139.	*Dauzonne contact – Timing*	*139*
140.	*Investigation evidence – Mrs Levistre*	*139*
141.	*White Fiat Uno – The authorities*	*140*
142.	*White Fiat Uno – Parameters*	*140*
143.	*Mercedes S280 – French inspection*	*141*
144.	*Henri Paul – Drinks consumed: Scotchbrook*	*141*

The Inquest **143**

145.	*Police inquest testimony*	*143*

ALAN POWER EXPOSED

146.	Attendance – French doctors	143
147.	Souad's attendance	144
148.	Dauzonnes' attendance	144
149.	Alain Remy – Non-attendance	144
150.	Video link evidence	145
151.	Evidence from paparazzi	146
152.	MI6 evidence in court	146
153.	Jury verdict	147
154.	Unlawful killing by following vehicles	148
155.	Dissenting jurors	149
156.	Inquest conclusion	150
157.	Inquest transcripts – Size	150

Other Issues 151

158.	Ritz Hotel – Location	151
159.	Michelle Blanchard – Laurent Relationship	151
160.	Gary Hunter's death	151
161.	Rees-Jones' book	152
162.	Karen MacKenzie – Occupation	152
163.	Landmines dossier – Size	152
164.	Nicholas Soames – Relationship to Churchill	153
165.	Nicholas Soames – Newsnight	153
166.	L'Hostis' statement	153
167.	Paul Burrell – Occupation	154
168.	Death of Queen Astrid	154

Word Manipulation 155

169.	"Uncontroversial" – "Incontrovertible"	155

Problems with Names...157

170.	Lord Justice Scott Baker	157
171.	Dodi Fayed	157
172.	Trevor Rees-Jones	157
173.	Georges & Sabine Dauzonne	158
174.	Martyn Gregory	158
175.	Kez Wingfield	158
176.	Nathalie Blanchard	158
177.	Sandra Davis	158

CONTENTS

178. John Stevens 158
179. Sarah McCorquodale 158
180. Dominique Lecomte 159
181. François Levistre 159
182. Brian Anderson 159
183. Olivier Partouche 159
184. Elisabeth Andanson 159
185. James Gilbey 159
186. Michael Messinger 159
187. Martine Monteil 160
188. John Macnamara 160
189. Souad Moufakkir 160
190. Mohammed Medjahdi 160
191. Alberto Repossi 160
192. Françoise Dard 160
193. Gerald Posner 160
194. JoAnn Grube 161
195. Vincent L'Hotellier 161
196. Aotal 161
197. Avenue des Champs-Elysées 161
198. Jonikal 161
199. Brigade Criminelle 161
200. Dis-Moi-Oui 161
201. Montpellier 162

The SAS Factor 163
Questions Around Authorship 167
Conclusion 171
Evidence, Maps, Diagrams & Photos 175
Bibliography 177
Author Information 181

Acknowledgements

I could not have written this book review without having previously carried out an eight year investigation into the deaths of Diana and Dodi, and writing the extensive *Diana Inquest* series.

So there is a long list of people who assisted me with that book series who have indirectly contributed to the completion of this review. I thank those people here but I won't relist them – their specific contributions have been recognised already in Parts 1 and 6 of the series.

I am incredibly grateful to my wife, Lana, who is my carer and has assisted with editing and ideas, and has also been a sounding board throughout the process of putting this review together.

During the compilation of this work I have encountered substantial electronic interference and this now makes me reticent to name anyone else who has helped directly with it.

Nevertheless I can say that I have had invaluable assistance from various persons in the United Kingdom during the research, writing and editing stages. To those people, who know who they are, I express my deep gratitude for their help.

Then finally, I must acknowledge the assistance of various people in different parts of the world who I requested to give me feedback on their opinions regarding the Power book. That was vital in my understanding of how the book was being perceived by those who seek the truth about what occurred.

Introduction

On Sunday 31 August 1997 Diana Princess of Wales and her lover Dodi Fayed died in Paris' Alma Tunnel in a suspicious car crash. Sixteen years later, on 29 August 2013, first-time author Alan Power published a book from the Isle of Man entitled *The Princess Diana Conspiracy: The Evidence of Murder*.

In his widely-publicised book, Power stated that Britain's Special Air Service (SAS) were involved in the 1997 killing of Princess Diana and orchestrated the car crash.

This extensive book review establishes that *The Princess Diana Conspiracy* is not only riddled with error, but also disturbing questions are raised about the true nature and purpose of the book.

ALAN POWER EXPOSED

Why This Review?[a]

Alan Power's *The Princess Diana Conspiracy* is primarily a work of fiction and fantasy, with actual facts interspersed throughout the book. It has fraudulently been presented and packaged as a product of lengthy investigative research that is full of truth-based facts.
This is not the case.
Power's book is a minefield of deceptive writing, manipulation of witness evidence, misinformation and misrepresentation of the facts surrounding the deaths of Princess Diana and Dodi Fayed.
There is a real risk that the huge amount of error in *The Princess Diana Conspiracy* could in the future be used to undermine the Diana conspiracy movement, and cause irreparable damage to the ongoing quest for the truth of what occurred in Paris on 31 August 1997.

That is the reason this book review had to be written.

The true case for the Princess Diana conspiracy to murder is based on an honest evaluation of the evidence – it has integrity and it is now I believe watertight. It is the people who still maintain it was just a tragic accident who have become the theorists. The reality is that the true evidence that Princess Diana was assassinated is so strong that there is no need at all to manufacture and alter evidence, yet it will be shown Power has done precisely that.

The Princess Diana Conspiracy has sold very well and has been widely read, particularly by those who seek to establish the truth. Its success was guaranteed by its timing of publication – in precisely the same timeframe as the MPS announcement that it was scoping new

---

[a] All underlining throughout this review is for emphasis by the author unless otherwise stated.

ALAN POWER EXPOSED

material on the crash: the SAS involvement revelations from Soldier N. This issue of timing of the book's publication is significant and it will be addressed later in this review.

Having already written nine investigative books on the subject I was stunned when I started reading *The Princess Diana Conspiracy* and realised the level of error on virtually every page. And I was even more shocked when later reading the reviews posted by ordinary readers on the Amazon UK site – "the facts speak for themselves"; "very precise facts described clearly"; "previously unknown detail"; "stating the true facts"; "meticulous in his research".

People have been falsely led to believe that the book is based on a decade – from 2003 to 2013 – of in-depth research. Power says that he has carried out "an extensive investigation" into the deaths and has "personally scrutinised over four million words of [inquest] evidence" (p188).

This review will reveal that Power's claims of such an exhaustive investigation of the evidence are fictional. And that his resulting work is so heavily flawed that it is detrimental to the search for the truth of what occurred in Paris in the early hours of 31 August 1997.

The hundreds of errors follow.

The Errors

All investigative books – I include my own – have some errors.
That is not the issue.
The issue here is the level and type of error.
There are so many errors in Power's "facts" in *The Princess Diana Conspiracy* that it becomes impossible for the reader to discern what is fact and what is fiction.

What follows is a list of just over 200 separate errors in the Power book, but given his propensity for repetition there are actually in excess of 500 errors altogether. Many are central to the understanding of the key events that took place.

However, this is not a comprehensive list of errors – I have addressed here only the ones that can be shown in a review of this nature. There are many more errors that are too complex to address here, despite their importance to the case.

Pre-1997[a]

1. **Diana and Charles' divorce**

Power: "Of course [Diana and Dodi] wouldn't set [an engagement] date before Diana's decree absolute came through on 29th August [1997]" – p7

"Charles and Diana's decree nisi [was] on 28th August 1996 [with] the decree absolute due on 29th August 1997, just before Diana was murdered and only hours before she could legally commit to Dodi Fayed" – pp22-23

"The Queen [ordered] a divorce in 1996 ... with the Decree Absolute that would have enabled Diana to remarry being granted just 36 hours before she was murdered" – p25

"The earliest that the couple can commit officially to each other is 30th August [1997] because [Diana's] decree absolute is to be finalised on Friday, 29th August, the day before [secret service agents intended] to strike" – p40

"Charles ... ceased to be Diana's husband literally just hours before her murder" – p56

"Diana [was] stripped of her HRH and ... left the royal family when her divorce from Charles Windsor was made Absolute on 29th August, just hours before she was murdered" – p229

"June 1997. Diana's marriage was over, with the Decree Absolute soon to be declared on 29th August" – p292

The Evidence: The copy of Diana and Charles' Certificate of Divorce (shown below) reveals that the decree nisi was on July 15 and the decree absolute was six weeks later on 28 August 1996.

---

[a] As shown later Power misspells a lot of names. Quotes in this review generally show the names as written by Power – the errors in the names are listed later.

ALAN POWER EXPOSED

Referring to the decree made in this cause

on the   15th   day of   July   1996,

whereby it was decreed that the marriage solemnised

on the   29th   day of   July   1981.

at the Cathedral Church of St Paul in the City and Diocese of London

between the petitioner and the respondent be dissolved unless sufficient cause
within six weeks from the making thereof why the said decree should not be
cause having been shown, it is hereby certified that the said decree was

on the   28th   day of   August   1996,

made final and absolute and that the said marriage was thereby dissolved.

Dated this   28th   day of   August   1996.

Figure 1

> Section of Diana and Charles' divorce certificate that shows
> the decree absolute was on 28 August 1996.
> Sourced from CNN website. The full text is at:
> http://edition.cnn.com/WORLD/9608/28/royal.divorce/decree/

Comment: Power makes several false statements.

a) He claims that the decree nisi was on 28 August 1996 – this is not true, the certificate reveals it was on 15 July 1996

b) He claims on six occasions that the decree absolute was on 29 August <u>1997</u> – it was actually 12 months earlier on 28 August <u>1996</u>

c) He claims that Diana lost her HRH title and "<u>left</u> the royal family" on 29 August 1997. This is also not true: the HRH title was removed on 28 August 1996, at the same time as Diana was <u>removed from</u> the royal family – she did not "leave" it, as such.

Power uses this erroneous claim of a 1997 decree absolute to add weight and drama to the timing of the Diana-Dodi engagement and the murder.

Although it is true that there was an engagement ring and an intention for Diana and Dodi to marry, it is completely false to state – as Power does – that the timing was dependent on the decree absolute. The divorce had clearly been finalised a year earlier, in August 1996.

2. Queen's order for divorce – Timing

Power: "The Queen [ordered] a divorce [between Charles and Diana] in 1996, one year before the crash" – p25

The Evidence: Paul Burrell, *A Royal Duty*, p220:
"A divorce was demanded by ... the sovereign.... A lengthy letter ... from the Queen ... arrived as a crushing blow on 18 December 1995".

Comment: Power places the Queen's order as "one year before the crash", or approximately August 1996. The order was made eight months earlier than that, in December 1995.

3. Loss of HRH title announcement – Timing

Power: "The public were informed on 5th September 1995 that Diana was to lose her HRH title" – p21

"The announcement on 5th September 1995 that, once divorced, Diana would lose her HRH status...." – p24

The Evidence: *New York Times*, 14 July 1996:[a]
It was "announced last week ... [by] Buckingham Palace ... [that] Diana would ... have to give up the right to use 'Her Royal Highness' before her name".

The Baltimore Sun, 13 July 1996:[b]
Diana will "no longer be called Her Royal Highness.... Princess Diana ... gave up her royal title in a divorce deal with Prince Charles that was announced yesterday."

---

[a] Sarah Lyall, *Her Royal Common-ness*.
[b] Bill Glauber, *Charles, Di Reach Royal Settlement*.

ALAN POWER EXPOSED

Comment: The announcement that Princess Diana would lose the HRH title was made on 12 July 1996 – three days before the decree nisi and over 10 months after Alan Power's fictitious date of 5 September 1995.

4. **Panorama interview - Timing**

Power: "On 20th September 1995 ... Diana stated on the famous Panorama TV interview that she would fight to the end" – p24

The Evidence: BBC Website, http://news.bbc.co.uk/onthisday/: "On this day 20 November 1995 ... Diana, Princess of Wales has spoken openly ... in a frank interview for the BBC's Panorama programme".

Comment: Power times the *Panorama* program twice in his book – first on page 24 quoted above and second on the following page, page 25, where he correctly states it as 20 November 1995.

On page 24 – where Power incorrectly says September – he ties that date in with Diana's loss of the HRH title, which he falsely claimed (see above) was on 5 September 1995. Power states that the loss of HRH would reduce the royal control over Diana and says "this was brought sharply to light" with the *Panorama* interview 15 days later. Power then goes further and says: "The announcement concerning [Diana's] HRH removal may well have prompted Diana to agree to the [Panorama] interview".

Both dates – the HRH removal on September 5 and the *Panorama* on September 20 – are fictitious.

5. **Diana's engagement ring**

Power: "Klein ... phoned Madame Ray, directrice of the Van Cleef & Arpels store [in Monte Carlo], to arrange a private viewing of some engagement rings and described what Dodi had told Klein he wanted to see, saying, 'There must be something ... with red or blue'. (Diana's blue sapphire engagement [ring] was bought there. It is the ring that Prince William recently gave to Kate Middleton" – p144

The Evidence and Comment: Diana's blue sapphire engagement ring was chosen by the Queen through the Crown Jeweller in early 1981 –

it was for the Diana-Charles engagement. Paul Burrell – who at the time was working for the Queen – describes the event on page 53 of his book *A Royal Duty*.

It is a Power fantasy that the blue sapphire engagement ring was purchased from a store in Monte Carlo.

6. **Lucia-Diana recording**

Power: "Gerald Postner ... had personally listened to recorded conversations between Diana and Lucia Flecha de Lima ... intercepted and recorded by the CIA" – p139

The Evidence: Inquest Transcripts, 28 Feb 08: 180.23:

Gerald Posner: Quoted from his 1999 article: "This spring in Washington I listened to ... [part of] an undated conversation between Diana and de Lima. The recording was made available by an active US intelligence asset, who says it was one of several collected by the National Security Agency."

Comment: The recording was made by the NSA – not the CIA as stated by Power.

Build-Up to Paris

7. Threat from Nicholas Soames

Power: "Diana ... accused [Nicholas Soames] of making threatening telephone calls to her when he apparently advised Diana that people can have accidents (having witness support at the inquests but denied by Soames)" – p17

"Nicholas Soames ... whom Diana accused of making threatening calls to her at Kensington Palace, with witness support at the inquests" – p78

The Evidence: Inquest Transcripts, 10 Jan 08: from 56.12:
Simone Simmons, a friend of Diana, described one phone call at Kensington Palace, when Diana beckoned her over to the phone and she heard a male voice threatening Diana – "accidents can happen". After the call Diana told Simmons that it was Nicholas Soames.

Comment: Power describes it as Diana accusing Soames and then this is corroborated by "witness support" at the inquest.

There is no separate evidence – outside of Simmons – of this threatening call. There is also no separate evidence of any accusation by Diana of a threatening call from Soames.

Power states the accusation was of "calls", plural. There is only evidence of the one call.

I am not suggesting this call didn't happen – the account from Simmons is compelling and credible, but the reality is there is no other account of Diana accusing Soames of a threatening call.

The closest to that is the evidence of Roberto Devorik who stated that Diana feared Soames.

Power has overstated the evidence and misled his readers.

ALAN POWER EXPOSED

8. Swan Lake performance – Venue

Power: "On 3rd June 1997 Diana was invited to a rendition of Swan Lake ... at London's <u>National Theatre</u>" – p292

The Evidence: The <u>Royal Albert Hall</u> website states: "On 3 June 1997 the Princess of Wales paid her last visit to the [Royal Albert] Hall, as patron of English National Ballet, to see Swan Lake" – <u>www.royalalberthall.com/about/history-and-archives</u> Click on "Timeline".

Comment: Power has wrongly stated the Swan Lake performance was at the National Theatre – it was actually at the Royal Albert Hall.

9. Dodi's Paris to St Tropez trip – Timing

Power: "On <u>15th July</u> [1997], Dodi who was in Paris .... flew down to St Tropez" – p4

The Evidence: Opening Remarks, 2 Oct 07: 36.6:

Coroner: "On the evening of Monday <u>14th July</u> 1997 ... Dodi travelled to join the [Bastille Day] party at the villa in Saint Tropez."

10. Diana's announcement

Power: "Andanson ... knew something was imminent with Diana because eight to ten days before arriving in Paris [Diana] had said 'great news was coming'" – p161

The Evidence: Opening Remarks, 2 Oct 07: 36.18:

Coroner: "An observation of Diana to journalists on 14th July 1997 that 'you're going to get a big surprise, you'll see, you're going to get a big surprise with the next thing I do'."

Comment: Power is wrong on both the content and timing of this announcement to the press made by Diana.

Power says 8 to 10 days before arriving in Paris on 30 August 1997. That would place it around August 21 – yet it occurred on July 14, over a month earlier.

According to Power, Diana said "great news was coming", but the reality is that she told the press that they could expect a "big surprise" from her.

BUILD-UP TO PARIS

11. St Tropez holiday – Diana and Dodi

Power: "Between 14th-20th July [1997] ... Diana and Dodi were staying at [Mohamed's] 'Fisherman's Cottage'" at St Tropez" – p148

The Evidence and Comment: The evidence is that Dodi arrived on July 14 and met Diana that evening. Diana was with William and Harry and the relationship with Dodi didn't commence until after they returned to London.

It is a Power fantasy that Diana and Dodi were together during this holiday. The full evidence of how the Diana-Dodi relationship developed is in the book *Diana Inquest: How & Why Did Diana Die?*

12. Diana and Dodi's relationship – Timing

Power: "When Diana found Dodi, it was ... pure heaven for <u>eight blissful weeks</u>" – p7

The Evidence and Comment: Diana and Dodi's relationship commenced after their return to London from St Tropez on Sunday July 20 and was terminated by the crash on Sunday 31 August 1997. Even if you take it from the day Dodi arrived in St Tropez – Monday July 14 – then that is a maximum of <u>under seven weeks</u>, not eight weeks.

13. "Kiss" Photo – Timing

Power: "The famous 'Kiss' photograph of 7th August taken on board Al Fayed's yacht" – p37

"Mario Brenna ... shot the famous 'KISS' photograph ... on 7th August 1997" – p283

The Evidence: Opening Remarks, 2 Oct 07: 38.18:

Coroner: "Dodi and Diana returned to England from that first cruise together on Wednesday 6th August 1997."

Comment: It is difficult to place a precise date for when Mario Brenna took the "Kiss" photo, but we can be certain that it wasn't on 7 August 1997 – the date chosen by Power.

It is known the photo was of Diana and Dodi on the *Jonikal* and it was published in the *Mirror* on August 10.

Diana and Dodi returned from their holiday on the *Jonikal* on August 6 and were in London together on the 7th, ahead of Diana's anti-landmine trip to Bosnia on the 8th of August.

The couple were not on the *Jonikal* on the 7th – as indicated by Power.

14. Engagement ring order – Timing and circumstances

Power: "On <u>22 August</u> our subjects [Diana and Dodi] order the engagement ring" – p40

The Evidence and Comment: Opening Remarks, 3 Oct 2007: 2.17:

Coroner: "The evidence suggests that the only opportunities to visit Repossi in Monte Carlo were on 5th and 23rd August."

There is substantial evidence that Diana and Dodi visited the Repossi store in Monte Carlo on <u>23 August</u> 1997. It was following this visit that Dodi contacted the Ritz in Paris, to ensure a specific engagement ring would be available at Repossi's Paris store at the end of the month.

The evidence is addressed in detail in the book *Diana Inquest: How & Why Did Diana Die?*

The affidavit evidence of an independent witness – a former journalist for the *Bild*, Trixi Chall – who saw Diana and Dodi at Repossi's Monte Carlo on August 23 – is at:

<u>www.princessdianadeaththeevidence.weebly.com</u>

Power suggests that both Diana and Dodi ordered the engagement ring – there is only evidence of the order being made by Dodi, not Diana.

Power is wrong on two counts – the ring order was not made on August 22 and it was not made by both Diana and Dodi.

15. Malibu property – Omission

Power, The Evidence and Comment: There were eight witnesses at the inquest – Paul Burrell, Michael Cole, John Johnson, Mohamed Al Fayed, Melissa Heming, Dorothy Umphofr, Stephen Griffiths and Lee Sansum – who indicated that Diana and Dodi would be living or spend time at Al Fayed's Malibu property.

BUILD-UP TO PARIS

Power has completely omitted any reference to Malibu in his book – instead he focuses on the Villa Windsor (mentioned eight times, e.g. p145) as a likely future residence, even though the balance of witness evidence indicated that would not be the case.

The evidence covering Diana and Dodi's future plans is addressed in detail in the book *Diana Inquest: How & Why Did Diana Die?*

16. **Richard Spearman's arrival in Paris – Timing**

Power: "Spearman took up his Paris post at the <u>end of July</u>" – p37

"Richard Spearman ... was posted to Paris <u>two weeks prior</u> to Diana's murder" – p76

"Spearman ... had been stationed [in Paris] <u>two weeks before</u> the attack" – p272

The Evidence: Paget Report, p767:

"Richard Spearman ... moved to Paris on Tuesday <u>26 August 1997</u>".

Comment: Other evidence reveals that the earliest it could have been known – via phone surveillance – that Diana and Dodi were travelling to Paris at the end of the month, was on August 18.

The date of August 26 for Spearman's arrival in Paris is confirmed in the 1998 Diplomatic List – a copy of which Richard Tomlinson provided to Judge Stéphan in Paris.

Power's conflicting accounts – an "end of July" arrival and "two weeks" before the crash – are both false.

MI6

17. Rogue elements in MI6 – Dearlove

Power: "Dearlove ... stated that it would be 'difficult, <u>but possible</u> for agents to act without the knowledge of the MI6 hierarchy'" – p69

The Evidence: Inquest Transcripts, 20 Feb 08: 93.22:

Mansfield (Lawyer): "I want to suggest that if there were elements of the security services who wanted to do something without your knowledge, it is not difficult. It was not difficult then, was it?"

Richard Dearlove (Head of MI6): "It would be very difficult to do.... It would be very difficult to do something, <u>if not impossible</u>, as I have described."

Comment: Power has replaced Dearlove's "if not impossible" with "but possible".

In doing this Power manages to change the meaning of what Dearlove was saying – and deceives the reader.

Dearlove was suggesting it was next to impossible – difficult, if not impossible – for rogue elements to act, whereas Power is quoting Dearlove saying it was possible for rogue elements to act.

Power went on to use this as a trigger for a major attack on Dearlove, and referred to "Dearlove's new 'evidence' that it could be rogue officers" who killed Diana – p70. In this process Power reuses the false "difficult but possible" quote four more times – pp71, 77, 232 (twice).

18. Assassination handouts – Miss X

Power: "We show that MI6 do kill people and are even issued with handouts on the subject" – p68

"Assassination handouts [at MI6 training] ... were ... inadvertently admitted to by Witness 'X'" – p80

"Extraordinarily [X] then slipped that there were no training manuals on assassination; only handouts!" – p89

ALAN POWER EXPOSED

"Remember, MI6 is an organisation that doesn't issue books on assassination techniques, only handouts" – p268

"MI6 ... don't have textbooks on murdering people, only handouts" – p284

The Evidence: Inquest Transcripts, 26 Feb 08: 138.6:

Mansfield (Lawyer): "In 1997 and going back to 1993 and 1992 ... was there [an MI6] training manual?"

Miss X (MI6 Administrator): "We did not tend to have a composite manual as such.... Different lectures would be given and different booklets would be handed out, papers and so on."

Mansfield: "Was there one on the use of force or the threat of force abroad in pursuit of certain objectives?"

Miss X: "I have never come across anything like that."

Mansfield: "No. So nothing was ever said in a document to anyone about the use of force?"

Miss X: "No."

Comment: Miss X stated that booklets and papers were handed out during MI6 training.

Power has twisted this to being a reference to "assassination handouts".

This is a complete misrepresentation of X's account – she went on to deny there was anything in writing about the use of force.

It is a theme of Power's handling of the MI6 evidence that he falsely attributed MI6 with admissions by them that they assassinated people. The reality is that MI6 do not readily admit to assassinating people and they certainly did not admit this at the inquest.

Power built on this false premise – MI6 admissions of killing people – to then conclude: "[MI6 witnesses] denied murdering people while at the same time admitting it, thus showing a justification for murdering Diana 'within their code'" – p95.

MI6

19. The Order Book – Mr E

Power: "'E' ... admitted that MI6 have a document called 'The Order Book', which describes <u>intended targets</u> and MI6 capabilities for engaging in <u>violent actions abroad</u>, including the use of SAS and SBS troops 'in addition to <u>other methods</u>'" – p92

The Evidence: Inquest Transcripts, 29 Feb 08:21.22:

Mansfield (Lawyer): "Was the charter for MI6 commonly known within the service as the 'order book'?"

Mr E (MI6 Controller of Central and Eastern Europe): "I believe so, the 'order book'."

Mansfield: "... Was part of the charter or order book ... that SIS/MI6 ... had to maintain a capacity and capability to plan and mount <u>special operations abroad</u>?"

Mr E: "Entirely possible, yes. I cannot remember this, but I think you are probably correct, yes."

Comment: Power states that E described the Order Book as containing information about "intended targets and ... the use of SAS and SBS troops 'in addition to other methods'".

E's evidence was that the MI6 charter – known as the Order Book – included information about MI6 maintaining a "capability to plan and mount special operations abroad".

There is nothing in there about "intended targets", "violent actions" or "in addition to other methods" – these are all a creation by Power.

Power has twisted E's evidence to exaggerate his account of the Order Book, at the same time deceiving his own readers.

20. Interviewing of Mr A – Dearlove

Power: "Dearlove ... said that when he heard one of his agents (Witness 'A' ...) had put forward this assassination plan, he 'believed' that he had interviewed him about it" – p81

"Dearlove, the boss, apparently needed to interview Witness 'A' over" the Milosevic proposal – p82

"[Dearlove] pathetically tried to suggest that he believed he interviewed Witness 'A' concerning this plan to murder Slobodan Milosevic" – p83

"Dearlove [said] that he interviewed Witness 'A' over his 'dreadful' assassination proposal ... another of Dearlove's dalliances with the truth" – p232

The Evidence: Inquest Transcripts, 20 Feb 08: 85.14:

Mansfield (Lawyer): "One of the most obvious things ... is to go to A and interview him and find out what on earth he thought he was doing.... So was he interviewed?

Richard Dearlove: "I am sure he was interviewed."

Comment: Dearlove stated that he was sure A was interviewed. Power has falsely claimed four times that Dearlove said "he believed he interviewed Witness 'A'".

Dearlove never claimed he interviewed A – just that he would have been interviewed.

21. Ephemeral and deniability

Power: "During these inquests MI6 used a description that well illustrates their thinking; 'ephemeral is deletable and deletable is deniable' – an excellent way of describing their tenebrous world" – p89

The Evidence: Inquest Transcripts, 26 Feb 08: 142.8:

Mansfield (Lawyer): "If something is ephemeral, it is deletable?"

Miss X: "Yes, it is, yes."

Mansfield: "If something is deletable, it is therefore deniable?"

Miss X: "It would depend on what you were talking about...."

Comment: Power has stated that MI6 used the description: "ephemeral is deletable and deletable is deniable".

These words – ephemeral, deletable and deniable – were only used once in concert during the inquest, and that was during the Miss X cross-examination shown above.

MI6

The excerpt reveals that this was a concept introduced by Michael Mansfield – not a description used by MI6, as falsely claimed by Power.

22. **Dearlove in Paris**

Power: "There was a large contingent of senior MI6 in Paris that weekend, including Dearlove" – pp69-70

"Dearlove, the [MI6] operations director ... was in Paris ... at the time of the 'accident'" – p87

"During the attack on Diana ... Dearlove ... was in Paris" – p233

"We know of Richard Dearlove's visit to Paris a few weeks before the murder and ... Richard Spearman ... was with Dearlove" – p272

The Evidence and Comment: There is no evidence indicating Dearlove was in Paris at the time of the crash. The evidence instead reveals that Sherard Cowper-Coles was the head of the operation in Paris – this is addressed in the book *Diana Inquest: Who Killed Princess Diana?*

On page 272 Power says "we know of Richard Dearlove's visit to Paris a few weeks before the murder" – yet this is the first mention in the book of it and Power provides no support for this.

23. **MI6 at British Embassy**

Power: "Some of these [MI6] agents were finally forced into admitting they were at the British Embassy in Paris that night" – p76

The Evidence and Comment: The reality is that not one MI6 officer or agent has ever admitted to being "at the British Embassy in Paris that night".

Power fails to state who admitted this – that is because no one did. Power has completely misrepresented the MI6 evidence – and deceived his readers – by claiming agents admitted being at the embassy on the night of the crash.

ALAN POWER EXPOSED

Power also wrongly states the people identified at the inquest as MI6 personnel were "agents" – they were actually officers. There were no MI6 agents declared as MI6 personnel at the inquest.

The officers generally do the planning and control of operations, and it is the agents who are employed to carry out the operative work on the ground.

The MI6 evidence is addressed in detail in the book *Diana Inquest: Who Killed Princess Diana?*

24. MI6 in Paris – Officer evidence

Power: "[Paris-based MI6 officers] couldn't remember where they were [or] what they were doing" on the night of the crash – p76

The Evidence and Comment: Every Paris-based MI6 officer at the inquest – Mr 6, Mr 5, Mr 4 and Ms 1 – provided an alibi, i.e. where they were at the time of the crash.

Other evidence indicates these officers were lying – addressed in the above-mentioned book – but Power has falsely stated that the officers did not provide alibis.

25. Richard Spearman – Inquest identity

Power: "Spearman, whom I believe was Witness I at the inquests" – p37

"Richard Spearman (I believe he was the witness known as H/SECT – Witness 'I')" – p76

"Witness I refused to answer virtually everything asked [at the inquest].... His name was not, of course, revealed but could it be Richard Spearman?" – p269

"We know of ... Richard Spearman, whom we believe was Witness 'I'" – p272

The Evidence: At the inquest the MI6 witnesses who were connected to Paris in August 1997 were denoted with numerals – 1, 4, 5 and 6. All other MI6 witnesses were denoted by alphabetic letters – A, E, F, H, I and X.

Inquest Transcripts, 29 Feb 08: 28.18:

Burnett (Lawyer): "In the [MI6] hierarchy ... in 1992 and 1993 ... you were on the central staff.... You were the private secretary to the chief, that is the head of MI6...."

Witness I: "I was."

Richard Tomlinson in his affidavit to Judge Stéphan: "Fishwick had annotated that the [1992] document be circulated to the following senior MI6 officers: ... Alan Petty, the personal secretary to the then Chief of MI6, Colin McColl."

Comment: At the inquest Witness I's testimony was primarily in connection with the 1992 proposal to assassinate Slobodan Milosevic. Witness I was identified as "private secretary to the ... head of MI6" in 1992-3.

In his 1999 affidavit Tomlinson identified the private secretary to the Head of MI6 in 1992 as Alan Petty.

This indicates Witness I was Alan Petty – not Richard Spearman as Power falsely alleges.

There is substantial evidence pointing to Richard Spearman actually being Witness 6 at the inquest – this is covered in the book *Diana Inquest: Who Killed Princess Diana?*

26. **David Spedding – Death**

Power: "Dearlove ... became [MI6] chief ... in <u>1999</u> after the sudden death of Sir David Spedding" – p76

The Evidence and Comment: Spedding died on 13 June <u>2001</u> – as Power correctly states later on the same page.

Power however is wrong here in stating Spedding died in 1999.

27. **Robin Cook – Death**

Power: "Cook mysteriously died at the age of fifty-eight on <u>15th May 2006</u>, not long before the inquests began" – p78

The Evidence and Comment: It is a matter of public record that Robin Cook died on <u>6 August 2005</u> at the age of 59.

ALAN POWER EXPOSED

So Power is wrong on two counts here – the date of death and Cook's age at death.

Ironically, had Cook died on Power's chosen date in 2006, Cook – who was born in February 1946 – would have been aged 60. Power would have still had the wrong age.

The Royals

28. Royals and the Law

Power: "The police ... are fully aware that the royals are bound by British law" – p118

The Evidence: The Official Website of the British Monarchy, www.royal.gov.uk/MonarchUK/QueenandtheLaw

Under the heading: How UK and EU law affect The Queen: "Civil and criminal proceedings cannot be taken against the Sovereign as a person under UK law. Acts of Parliament do not apply to The Queen in her personal capacity unless they are expressly stated to do so."

Comment: Power has falsely stated "the royals are bound by British law" – although other royals are bound, he fails to declare that the Queen is not.

29. Way Ahead Group – Chair

Power: "Prince Philip, the Queen's husband, chaired a committee called the 'Way Ahead Group'" – p107

The Evidence: Inquest Transcripts, 12 Feb 08: 4.8:

Burnett (Lawyer): "Who attended the Way Ahead Group meetings?"

Robert Fellowes (Queen's Private Secretary): "The Queen, the Duke of Edinburgh, their children, the Private Secretaries to the members of the Royal Family concerned, the <u>Lord Chamberlain, who chaired it with the Queen</u>, and the financial department, represented by the Keeper of the Privy Purse."

Comment: Power falsely stated Philip chaired the Way Ahead Group – it was instead chaired by the Queen with the Lord Chamberlain.

ALAN POWER EXPOSED

Henri Paul

30. **Henri Paul's General Duties - Driving**

Power: "Paul's regular duties included driving VIPs around" – p32

The Evidence: Paget Report, p163

Jean Hocquet (Henri's boss to June 1997): French Statement:
"It was not at all part of M. Paul's duties to drive cars, or to chauffeur people".

Inquest Transcripts, 29 Nov 07: 49.9:

Burnett (Lawyer): "Was Henri Paul employed as a driver by the Ritz?"

Frank Klein (Ritz President): "Not at all."

At 108.16: Mansfield (Lawyer): "As far as you were concerned, you were surprised that [Henri] was driving. Part of his role and his job description does not involve driving?"

Klein: "Not at all."

Inquest Transcripts, 31 Jan 08: 127.5:

Hough (Lawyer): "Did you think it was part of Henri Paul's regular duties at the Ritz to drive clients of the Ritz?"

Claude Garrec (Henri's best friend): "No, absolutely not."

Comment: The general evidence – Hocquet, Klein, Garrec – is that Henri Paul did not drive for the Ritz Hotel. Power falsely states the opposite – that he was regularly "driving VIPs around".

It is a significant reality that Henri was not a driver or chauffeur. This means that Henri's driving of Diana and Dodi for the final journey was actually an extremely unusual, and even unprecedented, event.

31. **Grande Remise Licence**

Power: "A rumour had been initiated from some source that Henri Paul wasn't licensed to drive the large Mercedes car but ... Klein confirmed that a licence is required only if a driver wishes to drive for hire or reward – that was not the situation here" – p142

ALAN POWER EXPOSED

The Evidence: Inquest Transcripts, 29 Nov 07: 130.8:

Horwell (Lawyer): "You have said that he did not have authorisation to drive the Mercedes."

....**Frank Klein** (Ritz President): "You need just a piece of paper from the Prefecture who says that you can drive –"

Horwell: "This is the authorisation?"

Klein: "Yes, but it is not a technical authorisation relating to the car. It is a technical authorisation which goes with a car hire company which are chauffeur-driven cars."

Inquest Transcripts, 4 Dec 07: 97.22:

Jean-François Musa (Owner, Étoile Limousines – hired the Mercedes out to the Ritz): "I was worried about Henri Paul driving. I knew he did not have a grande remise licence, the special licence to drive limousines, but I felt I had no choice.... There was pressure to say 'yes'. It was impossible to say 'no'. I do not know what would have happened if I had said 'no' but the consequences would not have been good for us as a company. The Ritz was our only client."

Comment: Frank Klein stated that Henri Paul didn't have "a technical authorisation which goes with ... chauffeur-driven cars" – which the Mercedes was.

The "authorisation" Klein was referring to is the Grande Remise Licence – Musa confirms that Henri did not have the required licence and that "worried" him.

Power has falsely stated:

a) that it was only a "rumour ... from some source" that Henri was not licensed to drive Diana and Dodi in the Mercedes

b) that "Klein confirmed that a licence is required only if a driver wishes to drive for hire or reward" – Klein said nothing of the sort and Power has made this up.

It is significant that Power doesn't mention Jean-François Musa – the person who owned the Mercedes S280 – at all in his book.

HENRI PAUL

32. **Henri Paul's Contacts List**

Power: "When police visited [Henri's] apartment after his death they found contact numbers in his phone book for the DST, the [RG], the ... DGSE ... and even the Elysée Palace, residence of the French President" – p34

The Evidence: Inquest Transcripts, 4 Feb 08: 56.9:

Hough (Lawyer): "On that list [of contact phone numbers] ... there are the names of various police officers ... [and] there is also an entry ... entitled "DST" with a name under it."

Inquest Transcripts, 31 Jan 08: 155.22:

Claude Garrec (Henri's best friend): "In addition to those on the list [of contact phone numbers] that clearly relate to the police ... 'RG' denotes the 'Renseignements Généraux', 'DST' denotes 'Direction de la Surveillance du Territoire'."

Comment: The British police showed Garrec Henri's phone contact list.

The evidence reveals the presence of contacts in RG and DST – but not DGSE and the Elysée Palace as falsely claimed by Power.

33. **Henri Paul's bank accounts**

Power: "Paul had about £300,000 in thirteen different bank accounts" – p59

The Evidence: The Paget Report (pp178-182) lists Henri's bank accounts and their balances. There were at least 15 accounts and the known balances totalled around FF1,250,000, which was about £125,000 at the time of his death.

Comment: Power has at least doubled the value of Henri's bank accounts.

34. **Aotal – Location**

Power: "In Henri Paul's apartment ... a packet of Ayotal tablets was found" – p225

The Evidence: Inquest Transcripts, 21 Jan 08: 137.23:

ALAN POWER EXPOSED

Hilliard (Lawyer): "We were talking about the empty packet of Acamprosate that was found in [Henri's] office."
Prof Robert Forrest: "Acamprosate or Aotal." [a]
Comment: An empty Aotal packet was found in Henri's Ritz office – Power wrongly stated it was in his apartment.

35. **Aotal packet**
Power: "A packet of Ayotal tablets was found" – p225
The Evidence: Paget Report, p173:
"Lieutenant Monot ... carried out a search of Henri Paul's office at the Ritz Hotel and found:
... One (1) empty pack Aotal tablets 333mg (in waste basket)".
Comment: The police found an "empty pack" – Power wrongly states it was a "packet of ... tablets".

36. **Aotal use**
Power: "A packet of Ayotal tablets was found that everyone knew did not belong to Paul. But perhaps the drug had been taken by the man lying next to Paul in the mortuary" – p225
The Evidence: Inquest Transcripts, 17 Mar 08: 109.18:
Hough (Lawyer): "The medications listed ... that M Paul purchased [on] ... 20th May 1997, two Noctamide, two Tiapridal, three Aotal?"
Vincent Delbreilh (Judicial Police Lieutenant): "Yes."
Comment: The police evidence showed that Henri Paul purchased Aotal from a pharmacy in May 1997.
Power has falsely claimed that "everyone knew [the Aotal packet] did not belong to Paul".

---

[a] Acamprosate and Aotal are the same drug.

Saturday, 30 August 1997

37. Paparazzi pursuit – Villa Windsor

Power: "The press ... never left the couple's side following them from the airport to the Ritz" – p38

The Evidence: Inquest Transcripts, 3 Dec 07: 12.22:

Burnett (Lawyer): "Is it right that you managed to lose the paparazzi on the way [from the airport] to the Villa Windsor?"

Philippe Dourneau (Mercedes 600 Driver): "Yes."

Comment: The general evidence is that the paparazzi lost track of the Mercedes carrying Diana and Dodi at about the time that it split from its back-up car. The Mercedes continued to the Villa Windsor, while the back-up car went to Dodi's apartment to offload luggage and personnel from the yacht. The paparazzi dispersed – some went to Dodi's apartment and some went straight to the Ritz.

There were no paparazzi around while Diana and Dodi visited the Villa, and also there were none following the Mercedes on the subsequent journey from the Villa to the Ritz Hotel.

38. Engagement ring purchase – Timing

Power: "Twelve days before the attack ... the engagement ring was purchased" – p264

The Evidence: Below is the receipt for the engagement ring purchased by Dodi Fayed from Repossi Jewellers – it is dated 30.08.97.

Figure 2

Comment: The engagement ring was purchased on the day before the crash – 30 August 1997 – not 12 days before, as falsely claimed by Power.

39. Henri Paul's movements between 7 and 10 p.m. – Alcohol

Power: "Two bartenders at Harry's bar ... said they saw Paul that night and that he drank two whiskies (the manager said that he wasn't there)" – p31

The Evidence: There was only one mention of Harry's Bar at the inquest – it was Henri's best friend, Claude Garrec, stating that Henri "frequented Harry's Bar in Rue Daunou". Garrec also stated that Henri frequented Willy's Wine Bar and the Bourgogne.

Comment: Power fails to name the two bartenders or the manager. The amount of alcohol consumed by Henri on the night is critical to this case – if it could be shown that Henri drank additional alcohol,

SATURDAY, 30 AUGUST 1997

then that would help the official case that he was drunk behind the wheel.

If the authorities – French or British – had witness evidence of Henri Paul drinking alcohol between 7 and 10 p.m., then they would have made sure that was heard at the inquest.

It wasn't.

It is not known where Power got this unsubstantiated and unsourced evidence, but it appears to be false.

40. Henri Paul's movements between 7 and 10 p.m. – Home visit

Power: "[Henri Paul] probably went home to his apartment ... since it was noted that he was clean-shaven when he returned to the Ritz and had changed his clothes" – p31

The Evidence: Inquest Transcripts, 4 Mar 08: 109.8:

Mansfield (Lawyer): Discussing the Ritz CCTV footage: "When [Henri Paul] ... returns to the hotel at 10 o'clock in the evening, it is clear, is it not, that he is wearing exactly the same clothes that he was wearing when he went off duty [around 7 p.m.]?"

Paul Carpenter (Paget Officer): "Yes."

Comment: The inquest evidence is clear: Henri Paul did not change his clothes. Yet Power states the opposite: "it was noted that he ... had changed his clothes".

41. Chez Benoît restaurant

Power: Diana and Dodi were "precluded ... from eating at Chez Benoît by ensuring a paparazzi reception" – p30

"The fact that the paparazzi were waiting for Diana and Dodi at the Chez Benoît proves others knew where they would eat that evening" – p30

"The paparazzi knew Diana and Dodi were going to eat at le Chez Benoît ... and then having harassed them at the restaurant, making it impossible for them to remain, they followed their Mercedes to the Ritz Hotel" – p38

"It was a simple matter [for the Secret Services] to inform the paparazzi of the couple's movements and guarantee a commotion outside the Chez Benoît restaurant to prevent [Diana and Dodi] from entering" – p46

"[At] Chez Benoît restaurant ... paparazzi were waiting there too" – p175

The Evidence: The evidence from the people involved – Philippe Dourneau, the Mercedes driver; Trevor Rees-Jones and Kez Wingfield, the bodyguards; Jean-François Musa, the driver of the back-up vehicle – is that the Mercedes went directly from Dodi's apartment to the Ritz Hotel. Dourneau stated that on arrival at the Ritz "there was a sea of people" – Paget Report, p210.

Comment: Power has created a false scenario of the Mercedes arriving at the Chez Benoît and Diana and Dodi being prevented, by the crush of paparazzi, from entering.

The reality is that the Mercedes went straight from Dodi's apartment to the Ritz.

42. **Meeting between Rees-Jones, Wingfield and Henri Paul – Location**

Power: "Trevor Rees-Jones and Kes Winfield were with Paul in the Hemingway bar at the Ritz that night" – p33

The Evidence: Opening Remarks, 3 Oct 07: 44.22:

Coroner: "Henri Paul ... joined the bodyguards in the Bar Vendôme."

Comment: The Hemingway bar, although it does exist, is not mentioned in any of the evidence for this case – it is not known where Power got this false information from.

43. **Henri Paul's condition – Willaumez-L'Hotellier**

Power: "Willaumez ... said that Paul had staggered into the head barman, Vincent l'Otelier.... Despite having no ... other evidence to support Willaumez's claim, the court still allowed this point to stand" – p143

SATURDAY, 30 AUGUST 1997

The Evidence: Summing Up, 1 Apr 08: 43.20:
Coroner: "Alain Willaumez ... [said that] when [Henri] left the bar, he clumsily bumped into Vincent L'Hotellier, but that is not borne out by Mr L'Hotellier, or the CCTV, which shows him leaving the Bar Vendôme in a normal manner."
Comment: Power says "the court still allowed" Willaumez's claim about Henri crashing into L'Hotellier to stand.
Baker actually said that the claim wasn't supported by witness or CCTV evidence.
Power's statement is false.

44. Henri Paul's role – Chauffeur

Power: "Henri Paul [was Diana and Dodi's] chauffeur for the night" – p1
The Evidence: Philippe Dourneau – Dodi's regular driver – picked up Diana and Dodi from Le Bourget airport and drove them around Paris throughout the afternoon and evening. It was Dourneau who chauffeured the couple from Dodi's apartment to the Ritz Hotel, arriving there at 9.50 p.m.
Henri Paul only drove for Diana and Dodi once – the final journey that left the Ritz about 12.18 a.m. and crashed five minutes later, at 12.23.
Comment: Power overstates Henri's driving role for Diana and Dodi – Henri was not their "chauffeur for the night".

45. Decoy Mercedes

Power: "Just before Diana and Dodi's departure, [Henri] Paul had another Mercedes drive to the front of the [Ritz] hotel as decoy" – p29
"Around midnight on 30th August a decoy vehicle drove round to the front of the Ritz" – p41
The Evidence and Comment: The Mercedes 600 had been used by Diana and Dodi throughout the afternoon and evening, with Philippe Dourneau – Dodi's regular driver – at the wheel. It was this car that transferred Diana and Dodi from Dodi's apartment to the front of the

Ritz, arriving at 9.50 p.m. From then on the Mercedes 600 stayed out the front and was later used as the decoy vehicle – it was not driven to the front "just before [the] departure", as claimed by Power.

46. **Diversionary manoeuvre – Darmon**

Power: "Darmon said ... Paul ... employed a diversionary manoeuvre by having a Mercedes drive around to the front of the Ritz" – p222
The Evidence: Inquest Transcripts, 29 Oct 07: 103.2:
Stéphane Darmon: "There was a strange sort of stunt in front of the hotel.... I think it was [Henri's] idea to stage the diversionary manoeuvre for the departure. He went to see the chauffeurs and then the Mercedes and the Range Rover left empty. Everyone was expecting them to go and collect the couple via the rear, but what happened was that the cars went around the square and returned and were positioned in front."
Comment: Darmon describes the Mercedes 600 – used to transport Diana and Dodi through the day – and its back-up car, leaving from the front of the hotel and doing a circuit of the Place Vendôme, then returning to where they had started.
Power has wrongly changed this account to "a Mercedes" simply driving "around to the front of the Ritz".

47. **Late Movements of Kez Wingfield**

Power: "After the 'accident', Mohamed Al Fayed produced a video, taken from the Ritz security cameras, that showed Diana, Dodi, Dodi's bodyguard Trevor Rees-Jones, another bodyguard called <u>Kes Winfield</u> and Henri Paul ... all leaving the hotel by the rear exit" – p32
The Evidence: The Ritz CCTV footage – shown at the inquest – reveals that Kez Wingfield left the hotel by the front exit.
Comment: Power has falsely stated that Wingfield left by the rear exit – the truth is he left by the front exit and travelled with the decoy vehicles.

SATURDAY, 30 AUGUST 1997

48. James Andanson's movements – Ritz Hotel

Power: "CCTV footage from the Ritz security cameras ... shows ... unidentified people watching outside the hotel during the ... evening. There was also a man who owned a white Fiat Uno ... reputed to be present. His name was James Andanson" – p38

The Evidence: Inquest Transcripts, 11 Mar 08: 153.3:

Pierre Suu (Paparazzo who was outside the Ritz): "If Andanson had been working in Paris that night, I would have known. He is not the kind of person to go unnoticed."

Comment: There has never been any credible evidence of James Andanson being outside the Ritz Hotel on the night of the crash – Power has falsely indicated that he was.

ALAN POWER EXPOSED

The Final Journey

49. **Route taken – Expressway**

Power: "One reason for ... why Henri Paul chose to drive to Dodi's apartment ... via the Alma was given as to avoid the traffic on ... the Avenue de Champs-Elysées. But ... we have evidence [from Levistre] there was very little traffic" – p206

The Evidence: Inquest Transcripts, 15 Oct 07: 82.14:

Burnett (Lawyer): "You drove ... to Cours Albert 1er, the service road.... Was there very much traffic around?"

François Levistre: "No, there was not a lot of traffic because it was the end of the holidays."

Inquest Transcripts, 3 Dec 07: 24.11:

Burnett (Lawyer): Was there any particular reason why you did not turn right and drive along the Champs-Élysées?

Philippe Dourneau (Driver of the decoy Mercedes): "It was a Saturday night and there is always a lot of traffic on the Champs-Élysées on a Saturday night, so it was a quieter road."

Inquest Transcripts, 11 Oct 07: 3.20:

Hilliard (Lawyer): "Perhaps the most direct route for you would have been along the Champs-Elysées?"

Thierry Hackett: "Absolutely."

Hilliard: "... Was there a reason why you did not take that route?"

Hackett: "Well, it was ... a Saturday night and usually the Champs-Elysées are a bit crowded with cars and people, so I changed my mind and I chose another route."

Comment: Power uses Levistre's testimony – that the traffic was quiet on the riverside service road – to suggest the reason Henri used the expressway was not because the Champs Elysées had heavy traffic. This is a twisted piece of logic.

ALAN POWER EXPOSED

The reason Henri went via the expressway was because the traffic there was quiet – this fits with Levistre – and also the Champs Elysées had heavy traffic on Saturday night – this fits with Hackett and Dourneau.

50. **Place de la Concorde**

Power: "The Mercedes managed to overtake all the stationary vehicles at the Place de la Concorde traffic lights and obtain a substantial head start" – p41

The Evidence: Inquest Transcripts, 1 Nov 07: 46.14:

Jean-Louis Bonin: "I was level with a large black Mercedes and on its left.... The Mercedes was behind a dark car and there was no one in front of me.... Then the lights changed to green and I started off normally, thinking that the car stationary in front of the Mercedes was not moving forward as if blocking it. Then, in my interior mirror, I saw the Mercedes which was pulling out and I heard its engine roar loudly and its tyres spin. I had done about 10 metres and was preparing to turn on to the embankments in the left lane when Diana's Mercedes overtook me at very high speed on the right."

Comment: Power's statement that the "Mercedes managed to overtake all the stationary vehicles" and had a "head start", ignores Bonin's clear evidence that a car was actually blocking the Mercedes. Bonin indicates that it was he who had the head start and the Mercedes overtook him just before the embankment.

Bonin's account is also supported by Stéphane Darmon, who was a paparazzo rider on a motorbike at the lights.

51. **Alexandre III Tunnel**

Power: "Alain Remy saw the Mercedes at the bridge prior to the Alma Tunnel; no other vehicles, including paparazzi, were in sight" – pxiii (Contents section)

"The Mercedes passed an inquest witness, Alain Remy, as it sped under the Pont Alexandre III. According to Remy ... there were no other vehicles in sight" – p41

THE FINAL JOURNEY

"Under the Pont Alexandre III Remy confirmed that a black Mercedes passed him.... At that point no other cars were in sight, either in front of the Mercedes or following it, confirming Darmon's testimony" – p189

"Under the Pont Alexandre III Alain Remy was overtaken by the Mercedes.... He didn't see any paparazzi vehicles" – p214

"Look especially at the evidence of Alain Remy, who confirmed that the Mercedes overtook him ... near the Pont Alexandre III, unaccompanied by other motor vehicles" – p225

"Remy saw the Mercedes speeding along the freeway by the Pont Alexandre III and there were no paparazzi in sight" – p242

"The very important witness Alain Remy ... said that ... after emerging from under the Pont Alexandre III (the one just before the Pont des Invalides) he was overtaken by a large black car.... At this point there were no other vehicles, including paparazzi, in sight" – p263

The Evidence: Inquest Transcripts, 17 Mar 08: 133.9:

Alain Remy: "I was between the two tunnels [Alexandre III and the Alma Tunnel] and I was ... overtaken by a large top-of-the-range car which was travelling at a very fast speed.... I must tell you that I am not a car specialist which is why I could not give you any details of the make of the car....

"Question: When this large saloon car overtook you ... did you see any other vehicles, cars or motorbikes following it closely?

"Answer: No."

Paget Report, p436:

Thierry Hackett (witness driving in the Alexandre III tunnel): "[The Mercedes] was clearly being chased by several, I would say between four and six, motorcycles. There were two riders on some of the bikes. These motorcycles were sitting on the vehicle's tail and were trying to get alongside it."

Hackett drew the following diagram for the French police on 18 September 1997.

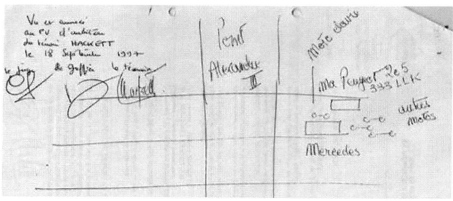

Figure 3

Hackett was cross-examined at the inquest on 11 October 2007 and stood by his account of pursuing motorbikes.
Inquest Transcripts, 15 Oct 07: 106.18:
François Levistre (witness travelling along service road parallel to the expressway before entering the expressway just before the Alma Tunnel): "We got on the avenue that is parallel to the piers. That is Cours Albert 1er.... I saw in my mirror, but from a distance, a car that was escorted on each side by motorcycles."
Comment: Hackett's testimony of pursuing motorbikes is supported by Levistre and other witnesses who saw one or more unidentified motorbikes along the route. The detailed witness evidence is in the book *Diana Inquest: The Untold Story*.
Power makes no mention of Hackett in his book and instead completely relies on Remy's account of there being no motorbikes. It will be shown below that: a) Remy is not a reliable witness on this; and b) Power has altered Remy's account to fit his scenario of the final journey.

52. **Exit before Alma Tunnel**
Power: "There is ... the suggestion that ... the Mercedes could have been prevented from exiting the freeway before the [Alma] tunnel by using a blocking vehicle. That however misses [a] crucial point.... The assassins drove fast behind the Mercedes ... to force it to maintain a high speed on entering the tunnel and ensure a fatal impact.... [Using

THE FINAL JOURNEY

blocking vehicles at the exit] just before the Alma, the Mercedes would need to reduce speed [to exit] and, on realising it was blocked, couldn't [then] regain sufficient speed [to achieve a fatal impact] as the [Alma] tunnel entrance is very close" – p246

The Evidence: Inquest Transcripts, 29 Nov 07: 170.15:

Frank Klein (Ritz Hotel President): "I go that direction, more than twenty years. There is an exit. After a long [Alexandre III] tunnel, there is an exit just off, opposite or in front of the Brazilian Embassy. Every, every person would exit there to go to the [area of Dodi's apartment]. There is no other solutions. If you go through the second [Alma] tunnel ... it is very difficult.... Henri Paul, who knows Paris very well, we all know this exit. You drive out there.... That was my first reaction: Why don't you exit here?"

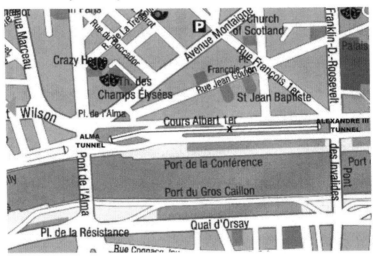

Figure 4

Map showing the route taken by the Mercedes S280 along the riverside expressway, after leaving the Alexandre III Tunnel. The intended exit is marked with an "X". It is approximately 700 metres from the Alexandre III exit to the Alma entrance – and about 400 metres from the intended exit (X) to the Alma entrance. Original map from Hot Maps: www.hot-maps.de

Comment: The issue here is that Power has concluded that Henri "chose to drive to Dodi's apartment ... via the Alma". His argument is that Henri's intelligence minders told him that he must go through the Alma Tunnel.

Klein's evidence reveals that no Parisian would actually go that way – they would take the exit before the Alma Tunnel to get to the area of Dodi's apartment.

Thierry Hackett's evidence – omitted by Power – raises the possibility that there could have been at least one motorbike on Henri's right that prevented him from taking the normal exit, marked with an "X" in the above map.

Power then says that the distance from the exit to the tunnel was too short for the Mercedes to regain speed before the tunnel. The key fact that Power omits is the actual distance between the exit and the Alma Tunnel – it as about 400 metres, which is ample distance for a Mercedes to increase speed.

Power has misled his readers into believing Henri wouldn't have tried to exit after the Alexandre III Tunnel, when all the available evidence indicates that is precisely what Henri would have done.

The full evidence regarding the route taken by the Mercedes is covered in the book *Diana Inquest: The Untold Story*.

53. **Alain Remy – Flawed Witness**

Power: "Alain Remy ... was ridiculed" – p242

Alain Remy's "crucial testimony was vigorously challenged" – p263

"The court proceeded to question whether Remy was even there and challenged his integrity by suggesting that it couldn't have been Diana's Mercedes [that he saw]. It was suggested that his memory of timing was in question because this testimony was fundamentally crucial.... Do we really believe a man would deliberately lie about such an issue?" – p264

The Evidence: Inquest Transcripts, 17 Mar 08: 133.2:

THE FINAL JOURNEY

Alain Remy: "I have a quartz clock in my vehicle and I noticed that the minutes column showed the number 35.... I cannot tell you if it was 11.35 on 30th August or 12.35 am on 31st August."

At 128.22: "a dark-coloured vehicle ... overtook me"

At 132.11: "my vehicle was overtaken by a large top-of-the-range car"

Summing Up: 1 Apr 08: 114.19

Coroner: "If Remy arrived at the scene at 12.35 am, which is the time he said his clock showed, that was later than the collision by some minutes.... Does this discrepancy ... suggest that the car that overtook him was in fact nothing to do with the accident? For if it was, Remy's evidence is worthless."

Comment: There are several reasons why Remy's evidence should not carry the weight that Power has assigned to it:

a) Remy's evidence about there being no vehicles close to the dark-coloured car that overtook him conflicts with every other witness, if it was the Mercedes that he saw

b) Remy never said that the dark-coloured car was a Mercedes – yet Power has repeatedly stated that Remy described a "Mercedes"

c) Remy indicated that he was overtaken by the car at 12.35 a.m. – that is 12 minutes after the crash occurred at 12.23 a.m.

54. **Alain Remy – Location**

Power: "at the bridge prior to the Alma Tunnel" – pxiii (Contents section)

"under the Pont Alexandre III" – p41

"under the Pont Alexandre III" – p189

"under the Pont Alexandre III" – p214

"near the Pont Alexandre III" – p225

"by the Pont Alexandre III" – p242

"after emerging from under the Pont Alexandre III (the one just before the Pont des Invalides)" – p263

The Evidence: Inquest Transcripts, 17 Mar 08: 128.19:

63

ALAN POWER EXPOSED

Alain Remy: "on coming out of the [Alexandre III] tunnel preceding the one at the Alma Bridge"

At 133.9: Remy: "I was between the two tunnels [Alexandre III and the Alma Tunnel]"

Comment: Remy clearly stated his location when overtaken by the dark car – he had already emerged from the Alexandre III Tunnel and was heading towards the Alma Tunnel.

Power has generally stated that Remy said he was "under the Pont Alexandre III" – this is a false statement.

The reason Power changes Remy's location will later become evident.

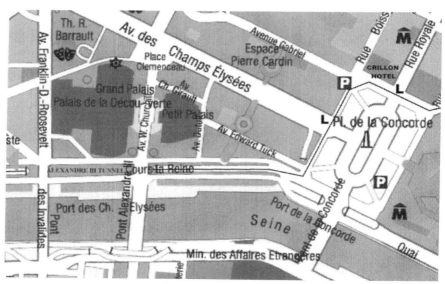

Figure 5

Route of the Mercedes S280 through the Place de la Concorde, onto the riverside expressway and through the Alexandre III Tunnel. This map shows that the Alexandre III Tunnel runs under both the Pont Alexandre III and the Pont des Invalides. Original map from Hot Maps: www.hot-maps.de

THE FINAL JOURNEY

55. **Pursuing motorbikes – Location**

Power: "Under the Pont Alexandre III Remy confirmed that a black Mercedes passed him.... At that point no other cars were in sight, either in front of the Mercedes or following it.... The attack vehicles lay in wait at the Alma Tunnel" – p189

"There were no vehicles near the Mercedes as it sped towards the Pont des Invalides [so] where did all the aggressive and pursuing motorbikes that witnesses reported ... come from?" – p190

"The attack bikes waited under the Pont des Invalides and on the slip road by the Alma Tunnel, from where they could quickly accelerate to begin chasing the Mercedes right into the tunnel; supported by witness evidence" – p190

"Vehicles can loiter on the road above [the service road] or near the slip road and then join the freeway at speed" – map caption on p190

"You will observe [from the map] that vehicles may wait on the road above the freeway [the service road]. The assassins started moving when they had a signal that the Mercedes was approaching.... They began the attack with vehicles that had considerable acceleration ... like the Turbo Fiat Uno and powerful motorbikes that several witnesses described" – p191

"The attack cars waited at the Alma entrance ... and the attack bikes were at the other side of the Pont des Invalides" – p214

"The [pursuing] bikes were probably under the Pont des Invalides and rapidly accelerated as the Mercedes approached" – p263

The Evidence and Comment: There are several points:

a)   Power has given different locations for where the pursuing motorbikes were located before they started chasing the Mercedes:

- "at the Alma Tunnel" – p189
- "under the Pont des Invalides and on the slip road" – p190
- "[the service road] or near the slip road" – p190
- "the service road" – p191
- "the other side of the Pont des Invalides" – p214

65

ALAN POWER EXPOSED

- "under the Pont des Invalides" – p263

In summary there are six locations Power puts forward: the Alma Tunnel; the slip road; near the slip road; the service road; under the Pont des Invalides and on the other side of the Pont des Invalides.

b)   Power uses Remy – a flawed witness (see above) – to show the pursuing bikes were not present in the Alexandre III tunnel. Yet Power falsified Remy's account to do this: he claimed that Remy was under the Pont Alexandre III when overtaken, but Remy clearly said he had already left the Alexandre III tunnel, so was between the Pont des Invalides and the Alma Tunnel (see map).

c)   Power then omits a very credible witness, Thierry Hackett, who was driving "in the first underpass by the Alexandre III Bridge" (Paget Report, p436). Hackett described being overtaken by the Mercedes "clearly being chased by ... between four and six motorcycles".

In summary, the evidence indicates the pursuing motorbikes joined the Mercedes at some point before the Alexandre III tunnel.

56. **Pursuing motorbikes: Number – Partouche**

Power: "[At the inquest] Partouche remembered he had seen more than one motorcycle travelling behind the Mercedes but when he gave statements to the police, only hours after the crash, he had confirmed seeing only one. Under cross-examination, the question was raised as to whether his memory was more likely to be accurate only a few hours after the crash than after ten years. Of course, MI6 would much prefer that this testimony indicated more than one motorbike because that would be the case if these vehicles were pursuing paparazzi. It would be more likely that there would be only one, or perhaps two, if these were in fact aggressive assassins with a very specific function: one behind to make the Mercedes go faster and one in front to deliver the deadly flash" – p203

The Evidence: Inquest Transcripts, 24 Oct 07: 6.7:

Hough (Lawyer): "Did you see anything on the expressway?"

Olivier Partouche: "... I saw a Mercedes car coming ... very, very fast and immediately followed by a number of motorcycles."

....Hough: "How many motorcycles?"

THE FINAL JOURNEY

Partouche: "A number. A number – I do not remember exactly."
....Hough: "You say also in your statement that behind the Mercedes there was a motorcycle."
Partouche: "Yes."
Hough: "Now, thinking back and reading that, do you think now that there was one motorcycle or more than one motorcycle?"
Partouche: "As I said, there was a number of motorcycles; not only one."
Hough: "You also say in your statement that you had the impression of a compact group. Could you describe that please or expand on it?"
Partouche: "... You could see a group, <u>a compact group</u>, with a car and motorcycles just behind."
Paget Report, p469
"Interviewed ... on 12 September 1997, Partouche ... said: "... behind the Mercedes there was a motorbike".
Comment: There are several issues:

a)   Partouche made five official statements and none of them were shown to the jury – only short excerpts were read out

b)   Power says that at the inquest Partouche recalled seeing "more than one motorcycle". Partouche actually said he saw "a number of motorcycles" and "a compact group with a car and motorcycles". It would be fair to suggest that Partouche here is describing more than two motorcycles, not just "more than one" as claimed by Power.

c)   Power states that Partouche described "seeing only one" motorcycle in statements taken within hours of the crash.

Partouche gave five statements – the first three were on the morning of the crash, the fourth was five days later on September 5 and the final one was on 12 September 1997 (24 Oct 07: from 1.22).

The Paget Report excerpt above reveals that Partouche's reference to seeing "a motorbike" was made 12 days after the crash – not "within hours of the crash" as claimed by Power.

d)   It is significant that neither Paget nor Hough provide the full context of this reference in Partouche's fifth statement to "a

ALAN POWER EXPOSED

motorbike". Paget makes no reference at all to Partouche describing a "compact group", even though the police also had that statement.

e)   We are not told when Partouche made the reference to seeing a "compact group", but it was quite possibly during the three statements made on the day of the crash.

f)   Power states: "Under cross-examination, the question was raised as to whether [Partouche's] memory was more likely to be accurate only a few hours after the crash than after ten years".

That never occurred – that is a Power construct.

All the lawyer said to Partouche was: "Thinking back and reading that, do you think now that there was one motorcycle or more than one motorcycle?"

g)   Power then deceitfully leaves out Partouche's answer.

Partouche said: "As I said, there was a number of motorcycles; not only one."

So Partouche insists on his account that there "was a number of motorcycles".

As suggested above there is a possibility that the "a motorbike" account has been taken out of context, by both Paget and Hough.

h)   Power then moves on to a very strange argument that really makes no sense at all.

First, Power fails to mention both of Partouche's key descriptions – "compact group" and "a number of motorcycles".

Second, he suggests MI6 would be happy with any witness account of more than one motorbike, because that would indicate paparazzi. And he says assassins would use a maximum of two motorbikes.

Power provides no support whatsoever for this and it appears to lack common sense.

It is logical that the Mercedes driver would feel more pressured if he was aggressively pursued by several motorbikes, as opposed to one or two.

It will be shown below that Partouche was not alone in describing the presence of a number of motorbikes.

THE FINAL JOURNEY

Other evidence indicates that the pursuing motorbikes were operating on the night as fake paparazzi – or "pursuing assassins posing as paparazzi" as Power himself appears to have forgotten he mentioned on page 29.

The full evidence regarding the pursuing motorbikes is addressed in the book *Diana Inquest: The Untold Story*.

57. **Pursuing motorbikes: Number – Anderson**

Power: "Andersen said ... the Mercedes [was] closely followed by two motorcycles" – p209

"Andersen saw two motorcycles pass him" – p242

The Evidence: Inquest Transcripts, 17 Oct 07: 98.11:

Burnett (Lawyer): "That was two motorbikes that you have mentioned. Was there any other motorbike ... that you saw?"

Brian Anderson: "Yes. There was a third one that came upon the rear of the car...."

Burnett: "Did that pass the taxi as well?"

Anderson: "They all three did, yes."

Burnett: "Was that also very close to the rear of the Mercedes...?"

Anderson: "It was close, but not as close as the other ones...."

Burnett: "In your statement you ... [say]: 'The bikes were in a cluster, like a swarm around the Mercedes.'...."

Anderson: "Meaning that there were four moving objects in close proximity and somewhat in concert in their movement forward."

Figure 6

Diagram made by Brian Anderson for the British police. It shows the 3 motorbikes – MC1, MC2 and MC3 – close behind the Mercedes (MBZ) as it overtook his taxi.

Comment: Anderson's clear account is that he saw three motorbikes around the Mercedes.
Power has falsely changed Anderson's account to only "two motorcycles".

58. Pursuing motorbikes: Number – Levistre

Power: "Levistre ... witnessed the Mercedes approaching the tunnel ... two motorcycles were close by" – p204
"Levistre saw <u>two motorcycles</u>" – p241
The Evidence: Paget Report, p455
François Levistre: 1 Sep 97 Statement: "I could see in the distance in my rear view mirror a vehicle surrounded on either side by motorbikes.... The convoy drew closer.... There were <u>more than two motorbikes</u>, travelling in tandem on each side of the car."
Inquest Transcripts, 15 Oct 07: 110.2:
Burnett (Lawyer): "Today you have told us that the first you saw of the motorcycle that caused the flash was just as you were entering the tunnel. Here [in your early statements], you speak of motorcycles long

THE FINAL JOURNEY

before."

François Levistre: "The lights of motorcycles, yes."

Burnett: "Where did those motorcycles go then on the account that you give?"

Levistre: "Well, one motorcycle."

Comment: Unfortunately Levistre provided confusing and conflicting testimony at the inquest, but his first account – made ten years earlier on the day after the crash – is very clear and likely to be his most accurate recall.

On 1 September 1997 Levistre said he saw the Mercedes "surrounded on either side by motorbikes" and "more than two motorbikes, travelling in tandem on each side of the car".

Power has falsely reduced Levistre's account to just two motorcycles.

59. **Pursuing Motorbikes: Number – Hackett**

The Evidence: Paget Report, p436:

Thierry Hackett (witness driving in the Alexandre III tunnel): "[The Mercedes] was clearly being chased by several, I would say <u>between four and six, motorcycles</u>..... These motorcycles were sitting on the vehicle's tail and were trying to get alongside it."

Hackett drew a diagram on 18 September 1997 (see earlier) showing the Mercedes and four motorbikes.

Comment: Power almost completely ignores Hackett's evidence in his book.

In fact Hackett – despite being a crucial witness – only receives one passing mention in the entire book, on p198: "The motorbikes seen to be aggressively following the Mercedes by two other witnesses (Thierry Hackett and Brian Andersen)".

60. **Pursuing Motorbikes: Number – Other witnesses**

Power: "Evidence from ... witnesses [other than Partouche] ... stated there were only one or two motorbikes" – p203

ALAN POWER EXPOSED

The Evidence and Comment: There is a theme in Power's handling of the evidence around the numbers of pursuing motorbikes.
Witnesses who saw more than two motorbikes – Hackett, Levistre, Partouche, Anderson – have either been omitted (Hackett), or had their evidence altered by Power (the other three, see above).
It is true that there were witnesses who saw only one or two motorbikes – e.g. Gooroovadoo, who was standing near Partouche. Partouche saw "a number" of motorbikes – yet Gooroovadoo describes just one.
The issue here is that the evidence from all the witnesses has to be looked at, and it is only then that one can reach an informed position on how many bikes were pursuing the Mercedes.
Another point to bear in mind too is that the events being described by witnesses were viewed in a matter of seconds, possibly only one or two seconds, or even less in some cases. One witness will see something that another witness didn't.
The full complement of witness evidence must be reviewed. Unfortunately Power has not done this. Instead he has arrived at a scenario of how it occurred – in this case, just one or two motorbikes. Any witness that doesn't fit this has been omitted or had their evidence altered.
Power has fraudulently claimed he has carried out a proper investigation of the witness evidence. The reality is that Power did no such thing.

61. **Mercedes' speed – Remy**

Power: "According to Remy the Mercedes was travelling at around 87-94<u>mph</u>" – p41
"Remy confirmed that a black Mercedes passed him at a speed that he estimated being between 87/94<u>km/hr</u>" – p189
"Remy was overtaken by the Mercedes travelling at a speed that he estimated to be between eighty-seven to ninety-four <u>km/h</u>" – p214
The Evidence: Inquest Transcripts, 18 Mar 08: 128.22:

THE FINAL JOURNEY

Alain Remy: "A dark-coloured vehicle ... overtook me on the left-hand side at great speed. I would estimate this as being <u>140/150 kilometres per hour</u>."

Coroner: "That would be <u>87 to 94 miles per hour</u>, I think."

Comment: Power has encountered difficulty in recording Remy's speed estimate for the Mercedes.

Initially he has it correct – 87-94<u>mph</u> (p41) – but in his other two references (pp189, 214) Power falsely states that it is 87-94<u>kph</u>. He has wrongly replaced the mph with kph.

62. **Darmon's speed**

Power: "Darmon said ... his speed was around <u>sixty to seventy</u> km/h" – p223

The Evidence: Inquest Transcripts, 29 Oct 07: 112.20:

Burnett (Lawyer): "In your statement, you say that you got to a speed of <u>between 80 and 100</u> kilometres per hour. Does that sound right?"

Stéphane Darmon: "Yes".

Comment: Power has falsely understated Darmon's speed – he has changed "between 80 and 100" kph to "60 to 70" kph.

ALAN POWER EXPOSED

Loitering Vehicles

63. **"Loitering" vehicles**

Alan Power refers to "loitering" vehicles 35 times in his book. 15 of those mentions show "loitering" in quotation marks (examples pp191, 198) – indicating that this word has been drawn directly from witness evidence.

The words "loitering", "loiter" or "loitered" do not appear once in the entire 7,000 pages of inquest transcripts. These words also do not appear once in the entire Paget Report.

Power has repeatedly deceived the reader by indicating witnesses described "loitering" vehicles, when they did not.

64. **David Laurent & Blanchard family**

Power: "David Laurent and the Blanchards. The whole family saw vehicles loitering as they approached the Alma Tunnel" – pxii (Contents section)

"David Laurent and the Blanchards witnessed two cars 'loitering' at the entrance to the Alma; one looked like a Fiat Uno and the other a slightly larger, dark car" – p191

"As David Laurent and the Blanchards] approached the Alma Tunnel, two cars were travelling very slowly" – p197

"These two cars were ... vehicles that had positioned themselves at the tunnel entrance, clearly having advance notice" of the coming Mercedes – pp197-8

"The cars were 'following each other closely' which indicates they were 'in it together' and were 'loitering' and had a collective purpose" – p198

"Laurent and his family [described] loitering vehicles" – p214

"Laurent said ... there were two cars loitering near the [Alma Tunnel] entrance" – p243

ALAN POWER EXPOSED

"Laurent said ... the [second car was] a larger, darker saloon" – p243
"Laurent considered that these vehicles were 'together', 'loitering' near the tunnel's entrance" – p245

The Evidence: Inquest Transcripts, 11 Oct 07: 52.18:

David Laurent: "Just before the [Alma] tunnel, I was surprised by a small car, which was driving at an abnormally low speed in the right lane.... It was an old model, light coloured, white or beige, a Fiat Uno type car."

At 53.13: "I continued on my way in the tunnel. I passed a second car, a ZX Citroen or R19 Renault-style Sudan, which was driving ... at a normal speed, 60 or 70 kilometres per hour."

Nathalie Blanchard (Laurent's Girlfriend): 11 Oct 07: 27.6: "Going down the [Alma] 'bridge' underpass. I remember ... I notice a small car driving slowly, maybe at 40 to 50 kilometres per hour in the right-hand lane. My boyfriend avoided it in the normal way.... [It] was light-coloured, beige, grey or white. I would say it was something like an Austin Mini or a Fiat Uno."

Lilian Blanchard (Nathalie's Father) 11 Oct 07: 33.1: "I think David overtook ... two cars at the entrance to the tunnel and finished overtaking in the tunnel.... I only know that both were light coloured.... They must have been small cars like Clios, R5s or 104s."

Gregory Blanchard (Nathalie's Brother): 11 Oct 07: 35.22: "I remember we went through a tunnel at one point and, as we came out, I heard a screech of brakes and a loud bang."

Michelle Blanchard (Nathalie's Mother): 11 Oct 07: 38.24: "Going under the Pont de l'Alma ... [Laurent] overtook on the right two cars driving one behind the other at normal speed."

Comment: David Laurent stated that he came across a slow moving car at the tunnel entrance and a second car "driving ... at a normal speed" that was further in the tunnel.

Nathalie concurs that there was a slow-moving car near the tunnel entrance.

Lilian and Michelle recollect overtaking two cars together that were travelling normally.

LOITERING VEHICLES

Gregory doesn't mention any cars.

Power has falsely misrepresented this witness evidence:

- Power states that Laurent described two loitering cars – Laurent only described one
- Power states the Blanchard family described two loitering cars – Nathalie described one; the other Blanchards did not describe any loitering cars
- Power says Laurent and the Blanchards described a dark car – there is no mention of a dark car in any of their evidence. Laurent, Nathalie and Lilian all referred to light-coloured cars

65. **David Laurent**

Power: "David [Laurent] said: 'I was taken by surprise, but even so, I had time to pull the steering wheel to the left to <u>avoid them</u>'" – p197

The Evidence: Inquest Transcripts, 11 Oct 07: 23.14:

David Laurent: "I was taken by surprise, but even so, I had time to pull the steering wheel to the left to <u>avoid it</u>."

Comment: Power has deliberately altered David Laurent's evidence – he has changed "it" to "them", claiming that Laurent had to avoid two cars when it was actually only one.

This then falsely strengthens Power's claim of multiple loitering vehicles near the Alma Tunnel entrance.

66. **Slip road**

Power: "The slip road was the logical place for assassins to lay in wait and Laurent described swerving to avoid vehicles on the slip road" – p245

"We know that other vehicles were on the slip road before the Alma Tunnel (Laurent entered from the slip road and described the loitering vehicles that he swerved to avoid)" – pp263-4

The Evidence: Inquest Transcripts, 11 Oct 07: 22.23:

ALAN POWER EXPOSED

David Laurent: "That evening I was driving ... along the embankment on the right bank towards Trocadero.... So I went through the Pont de l'Alma Tunnel to get to Trocadero".

Nathalie Blanchard (Laurent's Girlfriend): 11 Oct 07: 26.25: "We drove down Cours Albert 1er[a] coming from [Place de la] Concorde and going towards Trocadero. My boyfriend was going at about 80 kilometres per hour, I think in the right-hand lane, and we were going to come out at the Pont de l'Alma. As we were talking and doing a tour of Paris, we missed the exit and started going down the 'bridge' underpass."

Comment: Nathalie Blanchard reveals that they were intending to exit the expressway "at the Pont de l'Alma" – meaning the exit just before the Alma Tunnel.

This indicates that it is not possible for Laurent to have entered the expressway using the slip road just before the Alma Tunnel.

Power has falsely claimed that Laurent encountered loitering vehicles on the slip road before the tunnel.

67. Gooroovadoo

Power: Quoting Gooroovadoo in a "description prior to the inquests ... 'We saw two vehicles on the embankment'. [Power then adds] This latter observation was reported by others so again very difficult to ignore or sidestep. These could be back-up vehicles, positioned to collect injured personnel" – p203

"Gooroovadoo mentioned vehicles parked on the verge by the side of the tunnel" – p264

The Evidence and Comment: Gooroovadoo gave six statements to the French police and these were read out at the inquest.

The phrase on p203 does not appear in any of those statements and also Gooroovadoo never used the word "we" when making critical witness observations. Power fails to say where the quote came from.

---

[a] "Cours Albert 1er" can refer to either the expressway or the service road. In this case the context (below) reveals that Nathalie is referring to the expressway.

LOITERING VEHICLES

Power adds that unnamed "others" also observed these two vehicles – there is nothing in the witness evidence to support this claim by Power. Power has made this up to fit with his account about loitering vehicles.

68. **Number**

Power: "The loitering attack vehicles had all departed the scene, never to be seen again, except for the Fiat" – p42

"Witnesses described the Fiat [Uno] and several other vehicles 'loitering' at the tunnel's entrance" – p44

"Henri Paul [was forced] into going faster ... to meet loitering vehicles that all then vacated the scene" – p198

"These loitering and aggressive vehicles began the assault upon the arrival of the Mercedes. Some were waiting at the [Alma] tunnel's entrance.... We know that other vehicles were on the slip road before the Alma Tunnel (Laurent entered from the slip road and described the loitering vehicles that he swerved to avoid)" – pp263-4

The Evidence: Paget Report, p483:

Olivier Partouche (off-duty chauffeur standing near tunnel entrance): 31 Aug 97 Statement: "I could quite clearly see a dark coloured car travelling in front of a Mercedes limousine brake in order to enable a motorbike to draw level with the VIP vehicle [the Mercedes]."

Inquest transcripts, 12 Mar 08: 79.21:

Clifford Gooroovadoo (off-duty chauffeur standing near tunnel entrance): "The Mercedes was travelling behind another vehicle ... travelling at normal speed.... The Mercedes must have accelerated powerfully enough to be able to pull out and overtake that car."

Comment: Outside of the Blanchards and Laurent the only other witnesses to describe what could be "loitering vehicles" were Clifford Gooroovadoo and Olivier Partouche. They were standing close to each other and described one vehicle – a dark coloured car (Partouche) – that appeared to hinder the Mercedes' progress.

ALAN POWER EXPOSED

Put together with the Laurent-Blanchards evidence of the white Fiat Uno that gives a total of two vehicles witnessed loitering near the tunnel entrance – possibly awaiting the arrival of the Mercedes. Power though, by using the word "all" indicates there were at least three. He supports this on pp263-4 when he claims "some were waiting at the ... entrance' while "other vehicles were on the slip road". Power has taken witness evidence of a maximum of two loitering vehicles and turned it into something much bigger than what the witnesses described.

Alan Power:

"One cannot pick and choose evidence that suits a particular purpose" – page 270

In the Alma Tunnel

69. **Collision with wall before the Fiat Uno**

Power: Caption under photo of Alma Tunnel: "Picture the Mercedes glancing off the wall and striking the Fiat" – p193

The Evidence and Comment: All the evidence shows that the Mercedes entered the tunnel in the left lane – the lane closest to the pillars and away from the wall – and the initial collision was directly with the Fiat Uno.

It is a Power fantasy that the Mercedes glanced off the wall before the Uno collision.

70. **White Fiat Uno – Two impacts**

Power: "The Mercedes glanced off the Fiat Uno just outside the [Alma] tunnel ... however ... the Fiat struck again further inside the tunnel" – p44

"Based on close inspection of the evidence (shared in court by one police expert), it is my view that the assassin's initial intention was to block the recovery lane at the tunnel entrance and force the Mercedes into the pillars but this attempt failed and so he was forced to try again further into the tunnel" – p44

"This second impact [between Mercedes and Uno] must have been a rare 'accident' in any country's road history since it required a driver having hit a car once, to accelerate aggressively and pursue it in order to hit it once again" – p44

"The Mercedes was seen to straighten out after the initial collision, hence the need for further intervention by the Fiat" – p244

"The reason for the collision is that the Mercedes had escaped the first attack so the Fiat needed to pursue it and block it again.... Without this second manoeuvre the attack could have failed" – p258

ALAN POWER EXPOSED

The Evidence and Comment: Power produces two extraordinary and conflicting accounts. Up to page 244 he is talking about two collisions between the Uno and the Mercedes. Then on page 258 he changes this to the Mercedes dodging the Fiat's first attempt but colliding with it after the Fiat pursues it for the second one.

This is a very strange concept – the Fiat Uno hitting a Mercedes that is travelling at around 100 kph and then a split-second later catching up with it to hit it again.

In the investigations and inquest there was only ever evidence – witness and forensic – of one impact between the Mercedes and the Fiat Uno.

Power references a nameless "police expert" in court – but no expert at the inquest suggested that the Uno could have hit the Mercedes twice. This extraordinary claim – that there were two collisions between the Mercedes and the Uno – is a complete fabrication by Power.

This also raises doubts about Power's other claim that he made a "close inspection of the evidence".

71. **White Fiat Uno – Levistre**

Power: "Levistre saw a White Fiat and motorbike swerve in front of the Mercedes" – pxii (Contents section)

"Levistre was ... the only witness to initially mention a small white car from the attack scene – how would he know if he hadn't seen it since the police denied its existence for two weeks?" – p59

"Levistre described a small white car that the Blanchards, Souad and l'Hostis saw – and one whose existence the police refused to admit for a further two weeks" – p194

"Levistre saw two motorcycles and a white car; one motorcycle ... delivered a flash of light" – p241

"Laurent ... mentioned an old white hatchback at the tunnel entrance, as did Levistre" – p245

The Evidence: Paget Report, pp455-6

François Levistre: April 1998 statement to Judge Stéphan: "I was doing 120km/hr along the [service road].... I wanted to go back along

IN THE ALMA TUNNEL

the urban expressway at the entrance to the Alma Tunnel, so I looked in my [rear-view] mirror to see if there was anyone approaching.... I had seen the headlights of a car and of another car a little way from it, and the headlights of the accompanying motorcycles.... I accelerated in order to enter the tunnel. When I got to the hump just before the descent into the tunnel, one of the cars that I had seen overtook me. It was a white car, I do not know what make. It was a small car. I must have been travelling at 120 or 125 km/hr at that point, and I think he must have been doing 130. The white car went past. I am sure that there was no contact with that car. I continued driving through the tunnel". Levistre then went on to describe the prelude to the crash, the crash and the aftermath. He then says: "Reply to Question: I know Fiat Unos very well. At no point did I see such a car. I am positive that there were none there."

Comment: Levistre clearly recalled a white car driving at speed ahead of the Mercedes S280. Power has interpreted this to be the white Fiat Uno seen by other witnesses, even though:

- Levistre describes the white car overtaking him at 130kph before the tunnel entrance
- Levistre states the white car overtook him ahead of the crash occurring
- Levistre states categorically that he never saw a Fiat Uno.

Levistre saw a white car but it was not the Fiat Uno seen by Laurent, Nathalie, Souad, Boura and the Dauzonnes. The vehicle Levistre saw probably had no connection to the crash as it appears to have exited the tunnel ahead of the crash taking place.

Power has falsely twisted Levistre's account to make it appear to his readers that Levistre witnessed the white Fiat Uno which was involved in the crash.

72. **White Fiat Uno – Medjahdi**

Power: "Medjhadi saw a white Fiat Uno ahead" before the crash – p243

ALAN POWER EXPOSED

"Medjhadi ... reaffirmed that after the attack ... the Fiat then exited the tunnel at speed" – p243

The Evidence: Inquest Transcripts, 12 Mar 08: 114.12:

Mohammed Medjahdi: 31 Aug 97 Statement: "I do not think there were any vehicles between myself and the Mercedes.... I cannot tell you if there were other vehicles behind the Mercedes. My attention was focused on the Mercedes itself."

Inquest Transcripts, 6 Nov 07: 81.10:

Horwell (Lawyer): "Medjahdi was seen by the police and he made a deposition.... Do you know that he made no reference to having seen a white Fiat Uno?"

Souad Moufakkir: "That is right."

Comment: Medjahdi has never said he saw the white Fiat Uno. Power has falsely altered Medjahdi's evidence to claim that he did see it.

73. **Mercedes' movement after Uno collision**

Power: "The Mercedes was seen to straighten out after the initial collision, hence the need for further intervention by the Fiat" – p244

The Evidence: Paget Report, p486:

Benoît Boura: 17 Sep 97 Statement: "The Mercedes collided with the first vehicle that was in front of it and subsequently lost control and ended up crushed against the pillar."

Comment: Boura was the only witness who described the collision between the Mercedes and the Fiat Uno. He described the Mercedes losing control after the collision.

There was no witness evidence of the Mercedes straightening out after the Uno collision.

This is a Power construct.

74. **Cars witnessed – Boura**

Power: "Boura saw three vehicles approaching: two cars and one motorbike, in addition to the Mercedes" – p195

The Evidence: Inquest Transcripts, 24 Oct 07: 63.4:

IN THE ALMA TUNNEL

Croxford (Lawyer): "So [you saw] two cars and one motorbike?"
Benoît Boura: "Yes."
Croxford: "All ... coming towards you?"
Boura: "Yes."
.... Croxford: "The first car ... was dark coloured; correct?
Boura: "Dark colour, not black."
....Croxford: "The second car was the Mercedes, was it?"
Boura: "Yes."
Comment: Boura saw two cars including the Mercedes – just the Mercedes and one other dark-coloured car.
Power has falsely stated that Boura saw "two cars ... in addition to the Mercedes".
Boura's evidence is important but complicated – it is addressed fully in *Diana Inquest: The Untold Story*.

75. Horn – David Laurent & Blanchard family

Power: "David Laurent and the Blanchards ... all heard a horn that was followed by a loud bang" – p191
The Evidence: Inquest Transcripts, 11 Oct 07: 24.20:
David Laurent: "I heard an insistent hooting lasting about two seconds, then the sound of braking for two or three seconds and a loud crash".
Nathalie Blanchard (Laurent's Girlfriend): 11 Oct 07: 27.17: "I heard several noises, a fairly long burst on the horn, a squealing of tyres and a crash of metal".
Lilian Blanchard (Nathalie's Father) 11 Oct 07: 32.7: "I heard a fairly loud crash.... As far as I was concerned, I only heard that one noise."
Gregory Blanchard (Nathalie's Brother): 11 Oct 07: 36.11: "I did not hear a horn at any time."
Michelle Blanchard (Nathalie's Mother): 11 Oct 07: 39.6: "I heard a screeching of tyres. It sounded like someone braking, lasting two or three seconds. Immediately afterwards I heard a loud crash, muffled".

ALAN POWER EXPOSED

Comment: Out of the five people in Laurent's car only two – Laurent and Nathalie – heard a horn. Power has falsely stated that all five heard a horn.

76. **Bright flash – Witnesses**

Power: "Françoise Levistre – corroborated by several other witnesses – [described] a strong flash of light just before the Mercedes lost control" – p58

"Partouche, Gooroovadoo, Petel, Souad, Brian Andersen and François Levistre all saw this very bright flash" – p85

"The flash that Levistre saw was also witnessed by Brian Andersen, Boura, l'Hostis, Souad, Laurent and family, Petel, Partouche, Gooroovadoo and Brenda Wells" – p207

"[The court] had to concede a flash of light occurred because too many people witnessed it" – p209

The Evidence and Comment: Power creates a false picture of "many" witnesses seeing the bright flash.

The reality is that there were only three known witnesses to it – Brian Anderson, François Levistre and Souad Moufakkir. Their evidence is addressed in detail in the book *Diana Inquest: The Untold Story*.

Power has compiled two differing lists of people he claims saw the bright flash. In his first list, on page 85, he includes the three true witnesses – Anderson, Levistre and Souad – but also falsely adds Partouche, Gooroovadoo and Petel.

In Power's second list – found on page 207 – he relists those six but then falsely adds even more: Boura, L'Hostis, Laurent and family (Nathalie, Lilian, Michelle and Gregory Blanchard) and Brenda Wells. So, all up Power names 14 witnesses to an event that was only claimed to have been witnessed by three – Souad, Anderson and Levistre.

The evidence of Partouche, Gooroovadoo, Petel, Boura, L'Hostis and Wells is addressed below.

The inclusion by Power of David Laurent and the Blanchard family is quite astounding. They were well ahead of the Mercedes and didn't even witness camera flashes – consequently there is no mention of any kind of flashes at all in any of their evidence.

Power has altered and fabricated witness accounts to create an illusion of widespread witnessing of the bright flash. The truth is it was only witnessed by three people – all of whom were in a direct line with the Mercedes, Anderson behind and Souad and Levistre in front.

77. **Bright flash – Benoît Boura & Gaëlle L'Hostis**

Power: "Benoît Boura and Gaëlle l'Hostis observed this very violent flash of light as they descended into the tunnel from its other end" – p85

"Boura and ... l'Hostis ... were ... in the oncoming lane and on the other side of the pillars, when Boura observed very bright and 'violent flashes' of light ahead which, having been in the army, he immediately thought of as 'radar flashes'. When he had reached about one third of the way into the tunnel he ... 'heard the noise of the tyres, then an impact' ... thus indicating that these 'very bright' and 'violent flashes' occurred within the tunnel ... and only a moment before the Mercedes smashed into the pillars" – p195

"l'Hostis didn't witness the 'violent flashes' because she was asleep" – p196

"Boura, an army man, described the flash as being like a military strobe gun" – p241

The Evidence: Paget Report, p454:

Benoît Boura: 31 August 1997 statement: "I should add that before ... entering the tunnel, I saw flashes <u>in the distance</u>."

Inquest transcripts, 24 Oct 07: 43.24:

Hough (Lawyer): "Before you got to the tunnel, did you see any lights or flashes up ahead?"

Benoît Boura: "Before I got into the tunnel, yes."

Hough: "Can you describe what those flashes seemed like?"

Boura: "No, I could not say whether they were coming from speed cameras or ... they were just flash lights."

ALAN POWER EXPOSED

Hough: "Can you look please at [your] statement.... Do you see there, 'Les faits observes ...'?"

Boura: "Yes, violent flashes."

Hough: "Can you read the sentence beginning, 'Ayant ete chauffeur dans l'armee ...'?"

French Interpreter: "Having been a driver in the army, I thought right away that it could have been speed camera flashes."

Hough: "Now, it is translated in our translation as 'radar flashes'. Can you say whether you thought that they looked like speed camera flashes or some other kind of flash?"

Boura: "I could not say. According to me they were just flashes."

Hough: "Did you later connect those flashes with anything you saw subsequently in the tunnel?"

Boura: "Well, flashes from cameras used by photographers, but before ... I got into the tunnel and saw the photographers, I could not say."

....Hough: "In your statement, you told the police that you covered about a third of the tunnel without seeing any other flashes and then you started to hear some sounds. Does that accord with your memory now?"

Boura: "Yes, I saw flashes before I got into the tunnel and the crash when I was about a third of the way into the tunnel."

Inquest transcripts, 24 Oct 07: 71.6:

Hough: "On the approach to the tunnel, do you yourself remember seeing any bright or flashing lights ahead of you?"

Gaëlle L'Hostis: "No, because I was sleeping".

At 75.17: Hough: "As you were driving through the tunnel and as you were heading towards the Mercedes, did you see any bright or flashing lights at any time?"

L'Hostis: "No."

Comment: There are serious problems with Power's account of the Boura-L'Hostis evidence regarding flashes.

Power correctly states L'Hostis didn't witness flashes because she was asleep (p196) – yet earlier he falsely wrote "L'Hostis observed this very violent flash of light" (p85) and went on to strengthen this error

IN THE ALMA TUNNEL

by falsely including L'Hostis in a list of witnesses who observed the flash (p207).

Boura stated that he believed the flashes he saw were "from cameras used by photographers". Yet Power has proceeded to deliberately twist Boura's account:

- Power states Boura "observed this very violent flash of light", when it is clear that Boura saw flashes, plural
- Power says Boura saw the flash as he "descended into the tunnel", but it is clear from Boura's statement on the day of the crash that he was describing flashes he saw "in the distance" before entering the tunnel
- Power lies (p195) when he says Boura was already "on the other side of the [tunnel] pillars" when he saw the flashes
- Power introduces a complete lying fantasy when he states (p241) that Boura "described the flash as being like a military strobe gun" – adding false weight to his already false argument that Boura witnessed the bright flash.

In summary Power has comprehensively misrepresented Boura and L'Hostis' evidence regarding flashes – the reality is that L'Hostis didn't witness any flashes and Boura didn't witness the bright flash. Power has then proceeded to falsely add both of them to his fictitious list of witnesses of the bright flash.

78. Bright flash – Brenda Wells

Power: "Wells witnessed the crash and observed the flash coming from within the tunnel" – p85

"Wells ... witnessed the attack and saw the flash coming from the direction of the tunnel" – p241

The Evidence: 21 Sep 97 *Sunday Mirror* article quoting French statement:

Brenda Wells: "A motorbike with two men forced me off the road. It was following a big car [the Mercedes]. Afterwards in the tunnel, there were very strong lights like flashes. After that, a black car arrived. The big car had come off the road."

Comment: Brenda Wells – who was outside the Alma Tunnel in a car – described "very strong lights like flashes" coming from in the tunnel. She does not state whether this was before or after the crash.

Other witnesses in the vicinity of the tunnel described camera flashes or photographers immediately after the crash: Boura, Anderson, Da Silva, Samer, Richardson, Luz, Partouche and Gooroovadoo.

The bright flash that caused the Mercedes driver to lose control was a single flash – witnessed by three people (see above) – whereas Wells describes flashes, plural.

This evidence from other witnesses indicates that it was not the single bright flash that Wells saw – it was probably the camera flashes.

The evidence regarding the bright flash and also the camera flashes is addressed in detail in the book *Diana Inquest: The Untold Story*.

79. **Bright flash – Gooroovadoo & Partouche**

Power: "Olivier Partouche and Clifford Gooroovadoo ... witnessed ... flashes of light coming from inside the tunnel at the moment the Mercedes entered" – p191

"Partouche was asked about flashes and confirmed that he saw a powerful one coming from the tunnel ... as the Mercedes entered" – p202

"Partouche was outside the tunnel with ... Gooroovadoo when they observed the [bright] flash coming from within" – p241

The Evidence: Inquest Transcripts, 24 Oct 07: 23.7:

Keen (Lawyer): "You said ... [in] your statement given two hours after the crash: 'In front of the Mercedes was a car ... trying to make the Mercedes slow down....The object of this manoeuvre was to make it possible for the paparazzi to take photographs.'... Again, in this statement....: 'I saw flashes before the vehicles disappeared into the underpass.'

Olivier Partouche: Yes, sir.

At 37.19: Horwell (Lawyer): "You thought that the paparazzi were

IN THE ALMA TUNNEL

trying to take photographs of the people inside the car, is that right?"
Partouche: "Yes, sir."
Paget Report, p457:
Olivier Partouche: 31 August 1997 statement: "Then, after the accident, I saw numerous flashes coming out of [the tunnel]."
Inquest Transcripts, 12 Mar 08: 77.20:
Clifford Gooroovadoo: 31 Aug 1997 2.30 a.m. Statement: "I ... saw a motorbike with two people on it and also saw ... the pillion passenger ... taking one photo after another in the direction of the vehicle that was making the noise [the Mercedes]. The vehicles then disappeared into the tunnel and a few moments later I heard a tremendous noise [the crash]."
Comment: Power has again manufactured and altered witness evidence in order to claim that Gooroovadoo and Partouche, who were standing outside the tunnel, witnessed the bright flash – when they didn't.

The evidence from Gooroovadoo is that he saw photo flashes before the Mercedes entered the tunnel. Partouche also saw camera flashes before the tunnel and then after the crash witnessed camera flashes coming from inside the tunnel.

There are three main points:

- Power falsely claims that Partouche and Gooroovadoo saw "flashes of light coming from inside the tunnel" before the crash
- Power claims Partouche "confirmed that he saw a powerful [flash]" before the crash (p202) and that they both "observed the [bright] flash coming from within" the tunnel (p241) – Power has deceitfully and deliberately manufactured this account out of nothing
- Power has then falsely included these witnesses in his fictitious lists of people who saw the flash (pp85, 207).

80. **Bright flash – Erik Petel**

Power: "When [Petel] approached the Alma Tunnel, he saw flashing lights coming from within, which he presumed were car headlights, but could have been the strobe gun" – p216

Comment: Power uses a witness' description of car headlights from inside the tunnel to claim that it "could have been the strobe gun" – the bright flash.

Then Power takes this a step further and adds Petel to his spurious lists of flash witnesses on pages 85 and 207.

81. **Bright Flash – Levistre timing**

Power: "Levistre ... heard the crash and, at the moment, witnessed a bright flash of light" – p194

The Evidence: Paget Report, p455:

François Levistre: "There was a sort of big white flash. The [Mercedes] zigzagged to the left, to the right and to the left again".

Comment: Levistre saw the flash then saw the Mercedes lose control ahead of crashing.

Power has misrepresented Levistre's account by claiming he heard the crash at the same moment as seeing the flash.

82. **Jean Peyret – Speed**

Power: "[Jean Peyret] added that he was driving at about <u>fifty mph</u>" – p198

The Evidence: Inquest Transcript, 17 Oct 07: 37.21:

Jean Peyret: "I was not going very fast. I was going at a reasonable speed."

Hough (Lawyer): "What would you regard as a reasonable speed on that road?"

Peyret: "About <u>60 kilometres per hour</u>."

Comment: Jean Peyret stated he was going about 60kph – Power has altered this to 50mph, which is close to 80kph.

IN THE ALMA TUNNEL

83. Jean Peyret – Position

Power: "[Jean Peyret] added that he ... must have been at least fifty yards in front of the Mercedes" – p198

The Evidence and Comment: Jean Peyret made no comment in his evidence about seeing the Mercedes or how far in front of the Mercedes he was.

This is a Power construct, that M. Peyret said he was 50 yards ahead.

84. Sounds heard – Jean Peyret

Power: "[Jean] Peyret said ... he heard 'the sound of an impact and then, after that, another sound that was a much heavier, bigger, bigger impact.' He added ... 'The first [noise] sounded like car against car, but the second was a deeper sound, like a car ramming into a truck'" – p198

The Evidence: Inquest Transcripts, 17 Oct 07: 39.18:

Hough (Lawyer): "What sounds did you hear as you were coming out of the tunnel?"

Jean Peyret: "Well, first the sound of an impact and then, after that, another sound that was much heavier, bigger, bigger impact."

Hough: "I think you told the police that the sounds sounded like the crash of metal."

Jean Peyret: "Yes, I said that first of all I thought it was taking place overhead, on the bridge, and that it was in relation to a truck, a collision with a truck."

Comment: The first part of Power's quote of Jean Peyret is correct, but the part after "he added" has been manufactured – the only word that coincides with Peyret's actual words and context is "truck".

85. Mercedes' speed – Medjahdi

Power: Quoting Medjahdi: "[The Mercedes] 'was going very fast, I'd say at least <u>ninety km/h</u>'" – p201

The Evidence: Inquest Transcripts, 12 Mar 08: 110.20:

ALAN POWER EXPOSED

Mohammed Medjahdi: "I noticed a ... Mercedes.... I would estimate its speed as being at least <u>150 kilometres per hour</u>."
Comment: Medjahdi says 150kph – Power falsely changes this to 90kph.

86. 13th pillar
Power: "The Mercedes [crashed] into the pillars" – p239
The Evidence and Comment: The evidence is very clear that the Mercedes crashed into just one pillar – the 13th.
Power has misled his readers by claiming it crashed into "pillars", plural.

87. Motorcyclist's gesture
Power: "François Levistre saw a ... motorbike rider [dismount] and [make] a slitting-of-the-throat gesture" – pxii (in Contents section)
"Levistre ... saw <u>people</u> dismount their motorbike, look inside the Mercedes and make a slitting-of-the-throat gesture" – p194
"Levistre ... added that the two men ... stopped their bike [and] one rider dismounted and walked over to the [Mercedes and] made a slitting-of-the-throat gesture to his compatriot" – p205
"There was <u>no misinterpreting</u> ... [Levistre's] gesture of the slitting of a <u>human</u> throat" – p207
"[Levistre made] a slitting-of-the-throat gesture with his hands ... in court" – p208
"Levistre ... witnessed the rider dismount his bike and approach the Mercedes before making a slitting-of-the-throat gesture" – p241
The Evidence: Inquest Transcripts, 15 Oct 07: 96.11:
Levistre: "The motorbike stopped with two people on it.... The rear passenger [gets] down [off] the motorbike and goes to the car ... looks into the car ... and then the passenger looks at the driver of the motorbike and he makes a gesture with his hands, with both hands (indicates).... They go back on the motorbike and they drive on their motorbike."
Summing Up: 1 Apr 08: 109.16:

IN THE ALMA TUNNEL

Coroner: "The passenger on the bike went to the car and looked in, turned to his colleague and made a throat-cutting gesture to indicate what Levistre described as 'job done'".

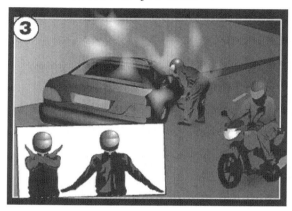

Figure 7

Diagram of gesture by motorcyclist correctly shown in *Daily Mirror* 16 October 2007

Comment: In October 2007 François Levistre made a gesture in court – shown diagrammatically in the *Daily Mirror* the following day – that indicated "mission accomplished".

The judge, Scott Baker, stated in his Summing Up six months later that Levistre had shown a "throat-cutting gesture" and had described it as "job done".

Levistre actually did neither of these things – he neither indicated a "throat-cutting gesture" and nor did he describe it as a "job done". Power – who concurs that Baker is corrupt – chose to describe the gesture as "slitting-of-the-throat" in line with Baker's false description. There are several points:

    a) Why did Power choose the "slitting-of-the-throat gesture" when the gesture made by Levistre was one that indicated "mission accomplished"?

95

b) Why does Power change his account on page 194 – he describes "people" (plural) making "a slitting-of-the-throat gesture"?

c) Power states on page 207 that there is "no misinterpreting" Levistre's gesture, yet he has gone ahead and misinterpreted it.

Power appears to deliberately sensationalise the gesture on page 207 – "the slitting of a human throat".

88. Mercedes' condition post-crash

Power: "The Mercedes ... eventually [came] to a halt, wrecked almost beyond recognition" – p42

The Evidence: Photos taken soon after the crash – before the top was removed to extricate Rees-Jones and Henri (both in the front) – reveal that the rear half of the Mercedes, particularly on the passenger side, was virtually unscathed.

Figure 8

Mercedes post-crash – passenger side

Figure 9

Mercedes post-crash – driver's side

Comment: The above photos reveal that the Mercedes was not "wrecked almost beyond recognition", as claimed by Power.

89. Diana's condition post-crash

Power: "Diana was reported by a paparazzo to be bleeding from the nose and ears" – p42

The Evidence and Comment: Power fails to declare which paparazzo said this and there is no evidence from any witness that there was blood coming from Diana's ears – although there was evidence of bleeding from her nose.

There was also no mention of any injury to Diana's ears in her post-mortem report.

Alan Power:

"Rest assured, my perception is not given to exaggeration or fancy but is based on the facts" – page 228

Fleeing Vehicles

90. **Fiat Uno post-crash – Souad**

Power: "As the Fiat overtook [Souad and Medjahdi] at speed, after the Mercedes crashed, Souad saw the driver's face" – p194

"The Fiat passed [Souad and Medjahdi] at speed after the attack ... and [Souad] saw the driver's face" – p200

The Evidence: Inquest Transcripts, 6 Nov 07: 79.2:

Croxford (Lawyer): "At some stage [the Mercedes] ... slewed across the road, was it?"

Souad Moufakkir: "Yes, it was going from left to right."

Croxford: "Your view of the road immediately behind the Mercedes was obviously obstructed by both the Mercedes and the white car?"

Souad: "Yes. That may be what happened, but I did not see the Fiat."

Croxford: "But at some stage before you left the tunnel, you saw these other cars in the distance on the slope, was it, coming in towards the tunnel?"

Souad: "That is right."

Comment: Souad's evidence is that she saw the driver of the Fiat Uno as it drew alongside her car prior to the crash. She stated to Croxford that she "did not see the Fiat" after that and has never claimed to have seen the Fiat after the crash occurred.

Power has falsely changed Souad's evidence to suggest that she witnessed the Fiat Uno pass her and saw the driver "after the Mercedes crashed".

91. **Vehicles – Lilian Blanchard**

Power: "As David [Laurent] exited the [Alma] tunnel, Lilian turned his head and saw the two cars emerge from the tunnel at speed" – p197

The Evidence: Inquest transcripts, 11 Oct 07: 33.16:

Lilian Blanchard: "When I heard the noise [of the crash], I turned my head to see what was happening. I saw the two cars we had just overtaken coming out of the tunnel."

Comment: Power has falsely added "at speed" to Lilian's account – apparently to use Lilian Blanchard as a witness of quickly fleeing vehicles, which he is not.

92. Vehicles – David Laurent & Blanchard family

Power: "David Laurent and the Blanchards ... witnessed vehicles fleeing from the tunnel at speed" – p191

"[Laurent's] passengers ... [said] they ... witnessed these [two] vehicles exit the tunnel at speed" – p243

The Evidence: Inquest transcripts, 11 Oct 07: 24.23:

David Laurent: "I looked back and did not see anything.... I did not see any vehicles coming out of the tunnel."

Nathalie Blanchard (Laurent's Girlfriend): 11 Oct 07: 27.21: "[After the crash] I turned round ... and I did not see anything, nor a crashed car or the small car."

Gregory Blanchard (Nathalie's Brother): 11 Oct 07: 36.19: "Right after we heard the crash, when we were coming out of the tunnel, I tried to turn round and see if I could see anything, but I could not see anything inside the tunnel or even outside."

Michelle Blanchard (Nathalie's Mother): 11 Oct 07: 39.8: "I heard a loud crash, muffled, and I thought there must have been a car accident. We carried on and came out on the right to get to Trocadero".

Comment: Power states that David Laurent and his four passengers – Nathalie, Lilian, Michelle and Gregory Blanchard – saw post-crash two "vehicles exit the tunnel at speed".

Lilian did witness two cars emerging – but not "at speed", see above. The evidence also shows that the other people in the car – Laurent, Nathalie, Michelle and Gregory – did not witness any cars.

Power has falsified the evidence of David Laurent and the Blanchard family.

FLEEING VEHICLES

93. **Motorbike – Peyrets**

Power: "Jean-Pascal and Séverine Peyret.... A motorcycle rider wearing a white helmet passed them at the end of the tunnel" – p194

The Evidence: Paget Report, p473:

"[**Séverine Peyret**] ... saw a motorcycle with one person aboard pass them at high speed.... The lone male rider of the motorcycle wore a light coloured crash helmet."

Inquest Transcripts, 17 Oct 07: 42.25:

Jean Peyret: "When we left the tunnel, Séverine ... has distinctively seen a motorcyclist that overtook us at a very high speed on our left.... I did not pay any attention to the presence of that motorcyclist."

At 40.14: Jean Peyret: "My wife saw something ... but I did not see a vehicle."

Comment: Power has altered Séverine's description of the colour of the rider's helmet from "light coloured" to "white".

This twisting of evidence has apparently been done to "match" it with accounts from other witnesses – see below. Yet it will be shown that the other witnesses – Boura, L'Hostis and Rassinier do not clearly describe a white helmet.

Power also falsely indicates the motorbike was seen by both the Peyrets – it was only seen and described by Séverine.

94. **Motorbike – Boura & L'Hostis**

Power: "Gaëlle L'Hostis & Benoît Boura ... confirmed the colour of the motorcycle driver's helmet as white and the fuel tank yellow, noticing both before it fled the scene" – p194

The Evidence: Inquest Transcripts, 24 Oct 07: 49.3:

Benoît Boura: "The motorcycle was ... the type of a 350 or 500 CC ... with a top case in the back, [or] a big scooter like the new model from Piaggio ... and round in the back."

Hough (Lawyer): "So it seemed like a low CC motorcycle or a Piaggio scooter. Is that right?"

Boura: "Yes."

Inquest Transcripts, 24 Oct 07: 74.25:

Hough (Lawyer): "You told the police ... that you saw a large motorcycle travelling behind the Mercedes. Do you recall that?"

Gaëlle L'Hostis: "Yes."

Hough: "You said that it was certainly not a Vespa scooter; it was a larger motorcycle."

L'Hostis: "That is what I said at the time."

At 84.19: L'Hostis: "[The large motorbike] slowed down fast ... and then accelerated and left."

Comment: Both Boura and L'Hostis described a motorbike – but apparently not the same one. Boura saw "a low CC motorcycle or a Piaggio scooter", whereas L'Hostis said she saw "a large motorcycle". Neither of these witnesses mentioned the colour of the helmet or the fuel tank.

Disturbingly, Power has:

  a) falsely stated that the Boura and L'Hostis' descriptions matched
  b) falsely stated that Boura and L'Hostis "confirmed the colour of the motorcycle driver's helmet as white and the fuel tank yellow".

95. Motorbike – Grigori Rassinier

Power: "Grigori Rassinier ... saw the motorcycle, confirming it had a yellow [fuel] tank" – p194

The Evidence: Inquest Transcripts, 22 Oct 07: 32.2:

Grigori Rassinier: "It was a fairly large motorcycle with a round yellow headlamp. I got an impression of white – I do not know if it was the helmet or the motorcycle's fuel tank.... This motorcycle left very quickly".

Comment: Rassinier describes a yellow headlamp and an "impression of white", which could have been either "the helmet or the motorcycle's fuel tank".

FLEEING VEHICLES

Power has falsely claimed that Rassinier saw a "yellow [fuel] tank" – he saw a yellow headlamp.

In summary:

a) No one saw a yellow fuel tank – but that has not stopped Power from falsely claiming that three witnesses did – Boura, L'Hostis and Rassinier.

b) No one described seeing a white helmet – the closest is Rassinier's "impression of white". Power has manufactured evidence from Jean Pascal Peyret, Séverine Peyret, Gaëlle L'Hostis and Benoît Boura – he falsely claimed they all saw a white helmet, which none of these people described.

c) Power has pretended that these five witnesses – Boura, L'Hostis, the Peyrets and Rassinier – have matching evidence about a fleeing motorbike. Although four of them saw a fleeing motorbike, their descriptions do not match.

Power adds on p212: "[Rassinier's motorbike] description fits in with other testimony, concurring even with the colour of the rider's helmet or tank". And this, on p220: "It's interesting how several witnesses describe the same or very similar events, even down to the colour of the motorcycle fuel tanks or riders' helmets".

As has been shown this claim of witness agreement on the colours of motorbike riders' helmets and fuel tanks is a Power construct.

It's not that Power is confused about the evidence. He reveals on p242 that he is aware of Rassinier's true account: "Rassinier saw ... a motorcycle with a large yellow headlamp and white helmet or fuel tank".

The full witness evidence about fleeing motorbikes is covered in the book *Diana Inquest: The Untold Story*.

96. **Motorbike – Jean Peyret**

Power: "Jean-Pascal Peyret ... spoke of being passed by a motorcycle seconds after the impact" – p221

The Evidence: Inquest Transcripts, 17 Oct 07: 40.14:

Jean Peyret: "My wife saw something ... but I did not see a vehicle."

Comment: Peyret specifically stated that he never saw the motorbike – yet Power falsely insists that he did.

97. Vehicles – Jean Peyret & Benoît Boura

Power: "Boura ... [and] Peyret ... confirmed that several vehicles had left the scene before the paparazzi arrived" – p221

The Evidence: Inquest Transcripts, 24 Oct 07: 61.22:

Croxford (Lawyer): "The vehicle [car] which had been travelling in the front of the Mercedes continued on its way; it drove off."

Benoît Boura: "Yes, absolutely."

At 65.18: Croxford: "Is this right, the motorcycle went round the left-hand side of the crashed vehicle, and carried on?"

Boura: "Yes."

Comment: Boura described just two vehicles leaving the scene – the car in front and the motorbike.

Jean Peyret witnessed no vehicles leaving the scene – see above.

Power has falsely stated that these two witnesses "confirmed that several vehicles had left the scene".

98. Gary Hunter – Timing

Power: "Hunter ... confirmed how only seconds after hearing a loud crash ... he ... witnessed two cars tailgating each other" – p244

The Evidence: Inquest Transcripts, 17 Oct 07: 23.19:

Gary Hunter: "At 12.25 am ... I heard the noise of an almighty crash.... I jumped out of bed and it was one pace to the open window. I looked to my immediate left.... I continued to watch for approximately a minute. I could not see what had happened.... I returned to the bed and lay down for what felt like a minute. It may have been less. I was then alerted by car noise in the form of tyres screeching at the bottom of the road.... I immediately returned to the window and looked left to see ... a small dark vehicle ... followed by a larger white vehicle."

Comment: Hunter described hearing the crash, getting out of bed, going to the window, watching for "approximately a minute", then going back to bed and lying down for another minute or less. Then he

FLEEING VEHICLES

heard the car noise and returned to the window and witnessed the two cars.

We are talking about around two minutes here. This is not the "only seconds" described by Power, who has altered Hunter's account.

Alan Power:

"Most of the evidence you have read in this book is proven" – page 275

ALAN POWER EXPOSED

Ambulance & Hospital

99. **Ambulance treatment – Omission**

Power: "When medics arrived, [Diana] was supplied with oxygen.... She was finally removed from the Mercedes and taken to the Pitié-Salpêtrière Hospital at 2.06am, although the ambulance needed to stop twice en route to apply cardiac massage" – p43

There is a possibility of "Diana not having received fatal injuries in the car crash but instead being murdered afterwards while still in the car or somewhere between the crash site and the hospital; perhaps even in the hospital. Fentanyl, in high doses, is a virtually traceless poison that has been reported to be used by the Security Services (it can be administered via a spray)" – p58

The Evidence & Comment: These two excerpts are the sum total of Power's comments on Diana's ambulance trip from the tunnel to the hospital.

There is substantial evidence – addressed in detail in the book *Diana Inquest: How & Why Did Diana Die?* – showing there was indeed foul play and mistreatment of Princess Diana inside the ambulance.

Power fails to address the huge time delay in treating Diana and the word "ambulance" only appears once in the book – excerpt above.

None of the doctors involved in the tunnel and the ambulance – Drs Mailliez, Martino and Derossi – receive any mention at all in the book. This is despite their extremely significant role in the events that took place.

In contrast, a doctor of considerably lesser significance, Dr Dion, receives 31 mentions.

100. **Ambulance stoppage en route**

Power: "[Diana's] ambulance needed to stop twice en route to apply cardiac massage" – p43

ALAN POWER EXPOSED

The Evidence: Paget Report, p515: 2004 Police Statement:
Dr Jean-Marc Martino (the doctor in charge in the ambulance): "I took that decision [to stop the ambulance] because the arterial pressure was dropping and I feared there would be another cardiac arrest. I had the vehicle stopped in order to re-examine the Princess.... I did not do any cardiac massage at that moment...."
Inquest Transcripts, 11 Mar 08: 150.12:
Pierre Suu (Paparazzo): "The ambulance stopped.... The hospital was only 300 to 400 yards away.... A doctor jumped out of the passenger side of the vehicle and rushed round the back of the ambulance and got inside. He was wearing a white doctor's jacket."
Inquest transcripts, 17 Oct 07: 13.4:
Thierry Orban (Paparazzo): "The ambulance stopped.... It was rocking, as if they were doing a cardiac massage."
Comment: All the witness evidence – from ambulance personnel and following journalists – was that the ambulance stopped only once en route to the hospital.
This is contrary to Power's false assertion that it stopped twice.
Dr Martino stated that he "stopped ... to re-examine the Princess" and did no cardiac massage.
Thierry Orban stated the ambulance "was rocking, as if they were doing a cardiac massage".
Power states that cardiac massage was applied – but provides no source for that. Orban indicates there could have been a cardiac massage, because the ambulance was rocking. But Orban was not inside the ambulance so couldn't be sure exactly what was happening. When the ambulance stopped there were already three staff in the back – Dr Martino and two female intern assistants. They were then joined by a second doctor from the front – Suu. There is a possibility – given the proximity to the hospital – that the stoppage was to carry out an action that would ensure Diana would not survive. Six minutes after arriving at the hospital Diana stopped breathing and never recovered. The evidence is covered in detail in the book *Diana Inquest: How & Why Did Diana Die?*

AMBULANCE & HOSPITAL

101.   Hospital Events – Timing

Power: "Diana's embalming ... took place around 2.00pm on 31st August, an hour before her body left the hospital to be transported home" – pp132-3

The Evidence and Comment: The general evidence is that the embalming concluded about 1.30 p.m. and Diana's body left the hospital around 6.15 p.m.

Power has wrongly said that Diana left the hospital one hour after the embalming – it was actually over four hours later.

102.   Dr Dion's affidavit

Power: "Dr Elizabeth Dion ... submitted a brief, non-committal affidavit" to the inquest – pxiii (in Contents section)

"Dr Dion [submitted to the inquest] ... a written affidavit ... that didn't say where she was on that fateful night" 30-31 August 1997 – p133

"Dr Dion gave a brief statement that didn't tell the court anything because it left out the crucial parts" – p215

"Dr Dion didn't say in her statement where she was on the night of Diana's death but only that she was resident in San Francisco. Was she visiting family or friends in Paris during August 1997?" – p215

"Dr Dion ... sent a sworn affidavit into court, saying merely that at the time of the attack she was working as a visiting professor in San Francisco" – p256

"Whereas we do not doubt Dr Dion's new appointment in San Francisco, what she omitted to do was confirm her whereabouts on the night of 30 August 1997" – p256

"People do go home for a holiday and August is a popular time for many – surely Dr Dion was in Paris that night?" – p256

The Evidence: Inquest Transcripts, 31 Mar 08: 5.4:

Dr Elizabeth Dion's statement read out: (also shown on p215 of Power's book).

ALAN POWER EXPOSED

"I, Elizabeth Dion, solemnly declare that on 30th and 31st August 1997, I was living in San Francisco, California, and working as a visiting Professor at the University of San Francisco California."

Comment: Power's argument is that Dr Dion has not stated where she was on the night of 30-31 August 1997 – "didn't say where she was" – and he emphasises this seven times throughout the book. In other words, Power indicates that by not declaring her whereabouts on the night of the crash, Dion is hiding her true location, Paris.

Yet if you carefully read Dion's short statement, she clearly states that on the weekend in question – "30th and 31st August 1997" – she was living and working in "San Francisco, California".

So what part of that statement does Power not understand?

This is not about whether Dion's statement is true or not. It is about what her statement says.

Power states that Dion <u>does not say</u> where she was. But Dion's statement <u>does say</u> where she was.

Power finishes up by asking: "Surely Dr Dion was in Paris that night?" The reality is that Dion's statement cannot be used to support the argument that she was in Paris – according to her statement Dion was in San Francisco.

103.   Locating Dr Dion

Power: "Sue Reid, a reporter ... discovered Dr Dion's whereabouts" – p215

"Isn't it strange that the police were unable to find Dr Dion" – p215

"The reason [Dion] wasn't 'found' [by the police] ... is because her evidence ... established a motive for murder" – p215

"It is strange that ... Detective Sergeant Philip Easton ... wasn't able to find Dr Dion; it fell to a ... reporter Sue Reid to do so and then Easton contacted Dr Dion ... by telephone" – p256

"The police were unable to find [Dr Dion] when a reporter did" – p256

"After the initial ... article Reid ... couldn't locate [Dion] a second time and so she informed ... Easton ... who managed to locate and speak with Dr Dion" – p215

AMBULANCE & HOSPITAL

The Evidence: Inquest Transcripts, 31 Mar 08: 4.10:
"Ms Reid had a meeting with an officer from Operation Paget on 22nd February 2006.... The [meeting] notes contain the following information ... [from] Ms Reid.... 'Sue Reid is unable to locate [Dr Dion].'... Easton contacted Dr Dion by telephone on 2nd and 12th June 2006."

Comment: The story is really simple – Sue Reid was unable to contact Dr Dion. She informed the police who then contacted Dion.

Power has turned this into: The police couldn't find Dion but Reid did find her. Reid told the police and Easton called Dion.

Power has actually reversed the roles – Sue Reid couldn't find Dion but he has stated falsely that she could find her; the police found Dion but Power has stated falsely that they couldn't find her.

Why has Power done this?

Apparently so he could make the claim: "The reason [Dion] wasn't 'found' [by the police] ... is because her evidence ... established a motive for murder".

There are a few other points:

a) in October 2013 Sue Reid confirmed to me that despite trying she was never able to find Dion

b) Power repeatedly refers to Sue Reid as a "reporter" – she actually is the Investigations Editor for the *Daily Mail*

c) the article Reid wrote does not name Dion – it refers to a "female radiologist". This is apparently because the information came from other sources – not directly from Dion herself. Despite this Power indicates that Dr Dion was named in the article (p215).

104. Jocelyn Magellan – Male nurse

Power: "[Frank] Klein ... received a phone call ... from a woman who was the aunt of a male nurse at the Pitié-Salpêtrière Hospital.... This woman ... gave the name of another nurse ... who had made a statement confirming Diana's pregnancy and gave it to the police. The

ALAN POWER EXPOSED

name of this nurse is Jocelyn Magellan and her address was.... She was going to meet with Klein but didn't turn up.... Klein said he believed she was from the French West Indies, either Martinique or Guadeloupe.... Jocelyn Magellan has not been heard from again" – p147

The Evidence: Inquest Transcripts, 29 Nov 07: 84.12:

Frank Klein (Ritz President): "I received a call at the hotel from a woman who said that she was the aunt of a male nurse at the Pitié-Salpêtrière Hospital who had been working there at that night. He had either seen a report or ... [information] that Diana, Princess of Wales, was pregnant. The name of this nurse was Jocelyn Magellan. The woman only gave me the name of the nurse and I checked in the telephone directory and found his address, which was...."

Burnett (Lawyer): "And the woman who called you did not leave her name?"

Klein: "No, she did not leave her name."

Burnett: "And she was going to come and see you, but she did not turn up at the meeting.

Klein: "No. And I recall that she was from the French West Indies, either from Martinique or from Guadeloupe, and she did not come. Most importantly, I had her address and I do not know what the French police did with her address.... I remember very well there was a meeting on – maybe scheduled on a Saturday afternoon, and then later she phoned me that she could not come or was unable to come because she flew back to the French West Indies, to Martinique or Guadeloupe."

Comment: Power changes various aspects of Klein's evidence:

a)   Power states: "This woman ... gave the name of another nurse". This is false – Klein said that the evidence came from the woman's nephew – not "another nurse". Power has made this up.

b)   Power states: This other nurse "had <u>made a statement</u> confirming Diana's pregnancy". This is false – Klein said the nephew "had either <u>seen a report or ... [information]</u> that Diana, Princess of Wales, was pregnant".

AMBULANCE & HOSPITAL

c)   Power states: This other nurse "had made a statement ... and gave it to the police". This is false – Klein makes no mention of anything from the nurse being given to the police.

d)   Power states: "The name of this nurse is Jocelyn Magellan and her address was...." Klein said that the woman's nephew was Jocelyn Magellan – a male nurse. Power has – by using the word "her" – falsely described a female.

e)   Power now transposes the role of the unnamed woman who contacted Klein – morphing her into a female nurse called Jocelyn Magellan. Power states: "She was going to meet with Klein but didn't turn up.... Klein said he believed she was from the French West Indies, either Martinique or Guadeloupe" – falsely indicating Klein is referring to Magellan.

f)   Power finishes with: "Jocelyn Magellan has not been heard from again". The reality is that Magellan was not heard from the first time – Klein was contacted by Magellan's aunt – not Magellan. There was never any contact between Klein and Magellan.

ALAN POWER EXPOSED

French Autopsies & Embalming

105.   Henri Paul autopsies – Witness evidence

Power: "The issue of whether Paul was drunk.... Some written <u>medical witness statements were read out</u> at the inquests, but only direct questioning of the doctors involved could have answered the pertinent questions" – p151

The Evidence and Comment: There were two autopsies conducted on Henri Paul's body.

The reality is that at the inquest <u>no statements were read out</u> from medical witnesses involved in either the pathology or the toxicology of either autopsy.

Power has falsely stated that some of these witness statements were read out at the inquest.

106.   Henri Paul autopsy – Second body

Power: "The corpse next to Paul was a car exhaust suicide – carbon monoxide" – p151

"The corpse in the same morgue as Henri Paul that night ... committed suicide by inhaling the exhaust fumes from his car (which would create high levels of carbon monoxide in the blood) – p155

"The man lying next to Paul in the mortuary you will remember ... had committed suicide by gassing himself with his car exhaust fumes that would account for very high levels of carbon monoxide in blood" – p225

"Remember the poor soul that had committed suicide by using his car's exhaust fumes and whose body lay next to Henri Paul's in the mortuary" – p260

The Evidence and Comment: Scientific testing has revealed that the minimum carbon monoxide level for a car exhaust fume death is

ALAN POWER EXPOSED

around 45%. Henri Paul's carbon monoxide level was stated to be 20.7%. This indicates that the second body would not have been a car exhaust victim – as falsely claimed by Power.

Other scientific evidence has indicated that the second body is most likely to have belonged to a fire victim with smoke inhalation.

This is dealt with in the book *Diana Inquest: The French Cover-Up*.

107. Henri Paul autopsy – Number mix-up

Power: "Major Mulès ... showed Paul's body as being No. 2146 when it was 2147 ... (the corpse next to Paul was a car exhaust suicide – carbon monoxide)" – p151

"Perhaps the suicide [victim's] body was placed next to Paul in the morgue and given the number 2146" – p155

The Evidence: Inquest Transcripts, 22 Jan 08: 5.13:

Keen (Lawyer): "Commander Mulès ... [wrote] at 08.20 [a.m.] on 31st August 1997.... He refers to an examination on the body of Henri Paul, IML reference 2146."

Prof Robert Forrest (Expert Inquest Toxicologist): "Yes."

Keen: "He might have been in error with regard to that number."

Forrest: "I think it's pretty clear he was."

....Keen: "Commander Mulès [wrote] at 06.45 [a.m.] hours on 31st August ... Dodi was registered at the IML under the reference 2147."

Forrest: "Yes."

....Keen: "Later blood samples [from Henri Paul] are recorded under a number 2147."

Forrest: "Yes, correct."

Comment: Mulès switched the body numbers between Dodi and Henri – Dodi's was 2146, but Mulès wrote it in error as 2147; Henri's was 2147, but Mulès wrote it in error as 2146.

Power has falsely suggested that the "car exhaust suicide" victim was the body involved in the Mulès number mix-up. This is not true – it was Dodi's body number that was mixed up with Henri's.

FRENCH AUTOPSIES & EMBALMING

108.   Second autopsy – Omission

The Evidence: Paget Report, p288:

Judge Hervé Stéphan (French Magistrate): "Order for appointment of expert. 4 September 1997. Appoint Dr Campana, Institut Médico-Legal. ASSIGNMENT: In my presence, to take the necessary samples, particularly of blood and hair, from the body of Henri Paul, currently held at the Institut Médico-Légal in Paris."

Comment: The second autopsy of Henri Paul's body was conducted on 4 September 1997 – four days after the first autopsy that occurred on August 31.

At the inquest the first autopsy and its results were shown to be corrupted, but it was claimed that the second autopsy results were more reliable.

Given that the authorities have relentlessly insisted that Henri Paul's drinking was the cause of the crash, Power's complete omission of Henri's second autopsy from his book is extremely significant. This is discussed below.

109.   Henri Paul BAC[a] result – Announcement

Power: "It's now known [Henri's blood-alcohol] results were not available when [the] police statement was given to the public. Yet the police still made the case for drunken driving" – p51

"It's proven [the blood test results] were not available between the crash and the police announcement that Paul was drunk" – p153

"It was proven that the police had emphatically stated Paul was drunk before they even had the results of his blood tests" – p222

"The police ... deliberately misled the people by issuing false statements concerning Henri Paul's alcohol levels before confirmation of Paul's blood results were received by them" – p238

"The police didn't have any blood results from Paul when they made their statement to the world that he was drunk" – p260

---

[a] Blood-alcohol concentration.

ALAN POWER EXPOSED

"Remember that the police had said Paul was drunk before they had even received his blood results" – p261

"It's known the police didn't have Paul's blood results when they proclaimed to the world that he was drunk" – p262

"We are shown that the results of any tests concerning the alcohol levels in Henri Paul's blood were not available to police when the world was told he was drunk" – p271

The Evidence: Paget Report, p302:

"The result of the blood alcohol test carried out by Dr Pépin's laboratory was formalised in a report dated 1 September 1997. He gave the blood alcohol level as 1.74 g/l.... Attached to Dr Pépin's report was an analysis chart timed at '13.19' [1.19 p.m.] on 1 September 1997."

Inquest Transcripts, 20 Nov 07: 50.16:

Weekes (Lawyer): "So on this day, 1st September, somebody ... issued a press release to the world's media saying that Henri Paul was three times over the alcohol limit when he was driving the car."

Maud Coujard (Deputy Public Prosecutor, Paris): "... It is the Office of the Public Prosecutor that issued that press release."

FRENCH AUTOPSIES & EMBALMING

Evening Standard (Final)
CIRCULATION 440,325
Monday, 1st, September, 1997
p. 1 - 2

DI'S DRIVER
'WAS DRUNK'

Sensational Paris revelation over 100mph smash

**from KEITH DOVKANTS in Paris
and SANDRA LAVILLE in London**

THE DRIVER of the car which crashed at 100mph killing Princess Diana was drunk, the Paris prosecutor's office said today.

In a sensational twist to the tragic story of Diana's death it was revealed that the driver, identified as Henri Paul, 41, was more than three times over the French legal limit and twice over the British limit.

The Paris prosecutor said M Paul, a Ritz security guard and not Dodi Fayed's regular driver, had a "criminally high" blood alcohol level.

Princess Diana and Mr Fayed's usual driver was switched at the last minute to drive a decoy vehicle when the couple were besieged by photographers outside the Ritz Hotel where they had been dining.

Throwing the whole debate about Press harassment into a new light, the prosecutor's office said this afternoon that M Paul, who lost control of the Mercedes car as it sped away from seven paparazzi photographers at 100mph, had a blood alcohol level of 1.75 milligrams per litre.

Figure 10

Comment: There are two points.

a)   Power consistently states that Henri Paul's blood alcohol level was announced by the police. This is not true – as Coujard and the

119

ALAN POWER EXPOSED

Evening Standard article above state, it was announced by the Paris prosecutor's office.

b)   The evidence from the Paget Report reveals the BAC result of 1.74 g/L was produced at 1.19 p.m.

During the afternoon an announcement was made by the Prosecutor's Office stating the result was 1.75 g/L.

The first UK newspaper report that the Mercedes driver was drunk – and quoting the 1.75 figure – was in the final edition of London's *Evening Standard* on Monday 1 September 1997 (shown above). The other London papers reported it the following day, September 2. Power's claim – repeated eight times in his book – that the police announced Henri was drunk before they had the results is false.

110.   **Autopsy results – Baker**

Power: "Scott Baker continually questioned the veracity of [Henri Paul's autopsy] results throughout proceedings ... and ... stated that the samples taken on 31st August are 'probably in doubt" – p154

"Baker ... said [in his Summing Up]: 'Even if you were satisfied that the 31st August sample had come from Henri Paul, you [the jury] would want to consider whether this inexplicable [carbon monoxide] reading causes you to have doubts about the whole process of analysis. If the carbon monoxide readings must be wrong, what about the alcohol readings...?' Yet this senior judge didn't tell the jury to ignore the blood sample evidence; why not?" – pp156-7

The Evidence: Summing Up, 1 Apr 08: 59.24:

Coroner: "Members of the jury ... you may want to consider whether, if there is any doubt about the results from [the] 31st August [autopsy], it is not safer to concentrate on [the] 4th September [autopsy]."

Comment: As mentioned above, Power omits any mention of the crucial second autopsy on Henri Paul's body.

Power states that Baker questioned the autopsy results, but deliberately and falsely omits to mention that Baker suggested to the jury that they should rely on the "safer" second autopsy results.

FRENCH AUTOPSIES & EMBALMING

In quoting Baker on p156 (see above) Power fails to show Baker's next words: "That is obviously a question you will want to consider, but again you will want to look at the whole spread of all the results, not simply the results for one substance from one day's blood. To do that would be to deprive yourselves of the opportunity of looking at the whole picture. Of course you must consider the details, but there comes a time when it is necessary to stand back and see whether or not it is clear what the overall picture establishes."

Baker's strategy was to let go of the first August 31 autopsy – it was clearly corrupt – but he clung onto the September 4 autopsy as being the reliable one.

Power's failure to admit this is more evidence of his deliberate attempts to mislead his audience.

The evidence around the two autopsies is addressed in detail in the book *Diana Inquest: The French Cover-Up*.

111.   **Henri Paul DNA tests**

Power: "We are left with the fiasco of ... blood taken for DNA tests that were not carried out" – p151

"The absence of DNA testing, which one presumes should have been of the utmost importance, was also unexplained" – p152

The Evidence: Inquest Transcripts, 6 Mar 08: 94.17:

Coroner: "The 31st August sample which was divided into three subsamples, that was examined for DNA by the French."

Prof Roy Green (Paget Forensic Biologist): "Yes, sir."

Comment: There is clear evidence that DNA testing was carried out – the problem with it was that it was conducted on different samples to the ones that were tested for alcohol.

The detail of this evidence is addressed in the book *Diana Inquest: The French Cover-Up*.

Power falsely maintains that "DNA tests ... were not carried out".

ALAN POWER EXPOSED

112. Diana post-mortem – In France

Power: "No post-mortem [on Diana] was carried out in France" – p56
"The French authorities did not carry out an autopsy on Diana to establish the cause of death" – p57

The Evidence and Comment: There is substantial evidence that Dominique Lecomte carried out post-mortems on both Diana and Dodi. This is addressed in the book *Diana Inquest: The British Cover-Up*.

Lecomte concluded that Diana's "death was due to ... a rupture of the pericardium and a wound to the left pulmonary vein": Forensic Report, Dominique Lecomte, 31 August 1997. This document is reproduced in the above-mentioned book and also in the book *Diana Inquest: The Documents the Jury Never Saw*.

Power has falsely claimed there was no "autopsy on Diana to establish the cause of death" in France.

113. Diana – Embalmer

Power: "Diana's embalming was carried out by Professor Dominique Lecompte" – p132

The Evidence: Inquest Transcripts, 20 Nov 07: 78.4:

Burnett (Lawyer): "Who, in fact, performed the embalming process?"
Jean Monceau (Embalmer): "Mrs Amarger, Josselin Charrier and myself, Jean Monceau."

Comment: The primary embalmer for Princess Diana in Paris was Huguette Amarger.

Power falsely claims that it was carried out by Dominique Lecomte, who was a pathologist.

James Andanson

114.   Vierzon – Distance from Paris

Power: "Andanson went on a ... trip ... to ... Vierzon ... [and then was] only 100km from Paris" – p254

The Evidence and Comment: Vierzon is around 200km south of Paris.

Power's account that the distance is 100km is false.

115.   Elisabeth Andanson's Paris trip

Power: "Mrs Andanson ... [drove] ... to Paris on the afternoon of Saturday, 30th August 1997 ... to seek a loan from her husband's boss, Hubert Henrotte.... Under oath, Elizabeth Andanson denied doing so in court" – p162

The Evidence: Inquest Transcripts, 21 Feb 08: 42.1:

Hough (Lawyer): "In the afternoon of that Saturday, is this right, you went to Paris to see Mr Henrotte?"

Elisabeth Andanson (Wife of James): "Yes, that is true."

Hough: "Was the purpose of your visit to persuade him to advance some money for your son's Formula 3 racing career?"

Elisabeth: "Yes, it was to talk about money in relation to this, yes."

Comment: Power has stated that Elisabeth Andanson denied seeking a loan from Henrotte. Yet the evidence shows that when asked in court she agreed with this.

116.   James Andanson – Corsica trip

Power: "[Andanson] produced airline tickets to show he had been at Orly airport.... He could have bought the tickets and not flown anywhere" – p61

ALAN POWER EXPOSED

The Evidence: The following two photos were shown at the inquest – 21 Feb 08: 57.22. The first shows Gilbert Bécaud, the singer Andanson photographed at his home in Corsica on 31 August 1997, in his living room. In the background the television is showing footage from the Pitié-Salpêtrière Hospital where Diana was taken. The second photo is a close-up of the TV set.

Figure 11

James Andanson's photo showing Gilbert Bécaud in his living room on 31 August 1997. The original can be viewed on the inquest website: photo reference: INQ-EMA100002.

JAMES ANDANSON

Figure 12

> Close-up of Bécaud's TV set. The original can be viewed on the inquest website: photo reference: INQ-EMA100004.

Comment: Power ignores the above photographic evidence – supplied by James Andanson's wife, Elisabeth, and shown at the inquest – indicating Andanson was in Corsica on 31 August 1997.
Instead Power states that Andanson "could have bought the [Corsica plane] tickets and not flown anywhere".

ALAN POWER EXPOSED

117. Corsica trip – Timing

Power: "Despite knowing Diana would be in Paris on the Saturday, Andanson claimed to have been going on a photo shoot assignment of Gilbert Bécaud ... in Corsica that day" – p161

The Evidence: Inquest Transcripts, 5 Feb 08: 32.21:

Hilliard (Lawyer): "The plane ticket to Corsica was bought at 6.23 in the morning on 31st August".

Comment: Power has falsely stated that Andanson's trip to Corsica was on Saturday, August 30 – it was actually a day later, on the 31st.

118. Corsica trip – Photos

Power: "Mrs Andanson remembered [James] had decided to sell his photographs from the Bécaud assignment of the 31st August in Corsica to the Sipa agency. They didn't materialise" – p162

"No photographs were ever received by the Sipa or Sygma agency from this supposed Corsica assignment" – p164

"Andanson ... didn't sell any photographs of his 'assignment' to Corsica, so do we believe he went there?" – p255

The Evidence: Inquest Transcripts, 21 Feb 08: 57.15:

Hough (Lawyer): "I think that in 2006 ... you collected photos from the Sipa agency.... Did you, among those, collect some photographs which you had asked for of the Bécaud assignment?"

Elisabeth Andanson (Wife of James): "Yes."

Comment: Elisabeth collected photos of the Corsica assignment from the Sipa agency – one of which appears above.

Power has falsely claimed that no photos were sold to the agency from this assignment.

119. James Andanson – Agency change

Power: "[Andanson had] recently decided to join the <u>Agence Angeli</u>, the best known celebrity agency in France" – p62

The Evidence: Inquest Transcripts, 21 Feb 08: 32.15:

Hough (Lawyer): "I think [James Andanson] worked for the Sygma agency for over 20 years before moving to the <u>Sipa agency</u> at the start of 17 September 1997."

JAMES ANDANSON

Elisabeth Andanson: "Yes, that is right."

Comment: The general inquest evidence revealed that James Andanson, after 24 years, resigned from the Sygma Agency on 5 September 1997 – five days after the crash – and started with the Sipa Agency.

Power has falsely indicated that Andanson was switching to the Angeli Agency.

120.   Agency change – Timing

Power: "Knowing Diana would soon be arriving [in Paris] ... it is hard to credit that any aspiring paparazzi would miss out on this news event especially since [Andanson] had just joined the hottest paparazzi agency in France" – p164

"Andanson ... [had on 30 August 1997] just joined a major paparazzi organisation specialising in this kind of [celebrity] work" – p254

The Evidence: Inquest Transcripts, 21 Feb 08: 8.14:

Hubert Henrotte (Head of Sygma Agency): "[Andanson] resigned on 5th September [1997]."

Comment: Power has falsely indicated Andanson switched agencies before the crash – Henrotte revealed his resignation occurred on September 5, five days after the crash.

121.   Andanson Fiat Uno Sale - Timing

Power: "The [Andanson] Fiat had been sold to a dealer in <u>October 1997</u>, just a month or so after Diana's murder" – p60

The Evidence: Inquest Transcripts, 7 Feb 08: 4.18:

Hough (Lawyer): "Could you look at the ... declaration of sale.... Does that document show that Mr Andanson sold the white Fiat Uno to you on <u>4th November 1997</u>? ...."

Jean-François Langlois (Fiat dealer in Chateauroux): "Yes."

Comment: Power states the Uno was sold in October but it was actually sold on November 4th. He uses the October date to claim that the sale occurred "a month or so after" the crash. The sale actually took place 2 months and 4 days after the deaths.

122. **Andanson Fiat Uno Condition**

Power: "Commander Mulès said that when he viewed the Fiat, it was on blocks" – p61

The Evidence and Comment: There was no evidence indicating Mulès ever saw the Andanson Fiat Uno. One of his staff Eric Gigou visited the dealership and drew up a report on the Uno's condition in February 1998 – that report is shown on page 710 of the Paget Report. There is no mention of the car being on blocks – instead there are descriptions of the condition of the wheels and tyres: "The front left tyre is practically smooth. The wheels are pitted with rust in places." Power is wrong on two counts:
  a) There is no evidence Mulès viewed the Fiat
  b) The police never claimed the car was on blocks.

123. **Andanson-Dards discussion – Timing**

Power: "Joséphine Dard reluctantly confirmed that her father had discussed the idea of writing a joint book about Diana's murder a few months before Andanson's 'suicide'" – p169

"Dard's daughter gave evidence that some weeks before her father's death he had discussed co-writing a book with Andanson" – p256

The Evidence: Inquest Transcripts, 6 Feb 08: 29.19:

Hough (Lawyer): Q. Your mother has told us about a conversation which took place with Mr Andanson in the Christmas holidays of 1997. Do you remember that?

Joséphine Dard (Daughter of Author Frédéric Dard): "Yes, I remember James coming. I could not remember exactly whether it was the Christmas of 1997 or 1998, but now I remember that he came for Christmas in 1997, yes."

Comment: Power has come up with two different claims regarding timing of the Andanson-Dard discussions:
  a) "a few months before Andanson's 'suicide'"
  b) "some weeks before her father's death"

JAMES ANDANSON

James Andanson died on 4 May 2000 and Frédéric Dard a month later on June 6. The discussion between Andanson and Dard took place around December 1997 – so that is about 2½ years before the two deaths.

Both of Power's claims then are clearly false.

124. Death – Distance from home

Power: "Andanson ... 'committed suicide' by driving 600 miles from his home ... where he burnt himself to ash" – p160

The Evidence and Comment: Andanson travelled from his home in Lignières, central France, to Nant in the South of France, where he died.

The distance travelled was around 240 miles – less than half of Power's claim. Had Andanson travelled 600 miles, he would have ended up in the middle of the Mediterranean.

125. Death – Timing

Power: "Andanson's 'suicide' [was] on 3rd May 2000" – p169

The Evidence: Inquest Transcripts, 7 Feb 08: 94.12:

Hilliard (Lawyer): "On 4th May 2000, I think you were one of a number of police officers who went to the scene of a burning car which had the body of a Mr Andanson in it. Is that right?"

Jean-Michel Lauzun (French police officer): "Yes, exactly."

Comment: James Andanson died on 4 May 2000 – a call to the fire brigade was made at 9.34 p.m. that evening (7 Feb 08: 95.16).

126. James Jnr's car racing costs

Power: "Andanson Jnr was an aspiring racing driver, a sport in which the costs and expenses are high (a figure of $300,000 per year was mentioned). This clearly indicates that his father was in need of funds way in excess of his earnings, which certainly illustrates motive" – p167

The Evidence: Inquest Transcripts, , 21 Feb 08: 65.9:

ALAN POWER EXPOSED

Hough (Lawyer): "At the time of his death, we have heard that your husband's income was high, around 2 million francs per year."
Elisabeth Andanson: "Well, I do not know that it was that high. I do not know who said that."
Hough: "Well, the French police concluded 2 million francs, £200,000 per year.... They also concluded from their inquiries that the cost of sponsoring your son's career at that time, [in] 2000, was over 700,000 francs per year; over one-third of your husband's income."
Elisabeth: "No, it was not that. It is not the figures that I have in mind.... It was much less.... It was not at all as much as this."
Comment: Two figures were put forward:
-   "700,000 francs per year" for James Jnr's career costs
-   "2 million francs, £200,000 per year" for James Snr's income.
In US dollars, which is what Power uses, these figures would in 1997 equate to approximately $140,000 for the career costs and $400,000 for the income – (exchange rate of 5FF to $1 and 50p to $1).
In 2012 to 2013 – when Power probably wrote his book – the FF was no longer in use, but the exchange rate for the £ to $ was hovering between 62-64p to $1. £200,000 converted in this period would equate to around $US317,000.
It is likely that Power has taken the figure quoted for James Snr's income – £200,000 – and falsely used it to calculate the $US equivalent for James Jnr's career costs. He appears to have arrived at $317,000 and has rounded this to end up with a figure of $300,000.
In doing this Power has made two errors:
   a) He has used the figure for James Snr's income and misrepresented it as being for James Jnr's career costs
   b) He has converted the currencies using 2012-3 exchange rates rather than doing it for the relevant time period – 1997.
As a result of this flawed process, Power has arrived at a figure of $300,000 a year for Jnr's suggested career costs, instead of $140,000. Power has then used this inflated figure to help provide Andanson's motive for involvement in the crash – "his father was in need of funds". Power then further misleads his readers by claiming that the

JAMES ANDANSON

$300,000 was "way in excess of [Snr's] earnings" – when the figure Power has calculated is wrongly <u>based on the suggested earnings</u> for James Snr.

127. **Philippe Poincloux**

Power: "When asked, [Andanson's] son said he didn't know Poincloux" – p168

The Evidence: Inquest Transcripts, 21 Feb 08: 100.20:

Mansfield (Lawyer): "Are you familiar with this name ... Philippe Poincloux?"

James Andanson Jnr: "Philippe Poincloux, it does not ring a bell, no."

Mansfield: "I just follow it with one question. Your mother told the juge conducting the investigation that he, Philippe Poincloux, had received a telephone call on Thursday, 4th May.... Does the name mean anything to you?

James Andanson Jnr: "Yes, it does. It is the one who introduced Luc Alphan in motor racing. The name of the association I cannot remember."

Comment: Power has stated James Jnr didn't know Poincloux, when it appears he did.

128. **Inquest handling of Andanson**

Power: "The court ruled that the consideration of James Andanson was 'not appropriate to these proceedings'" – p111

"The court declared that Andanson was 'not appropriate to these proceedings'" – p159

"Remember, the court declared [Andanson] 'inappropriate to these proceedings'" – p170

"The court ruled that Andanson 'had nothing to do with these proceedings'" – p210

ALAN POWER EXPOSED

The Evidence and Comment: There is no evidence of the court making a ruling of this nature – "not appropriate to these proceedings" – regarding Andanson.

The reality is that in Baker's final Summing Up to the jury he addressed Andanson in detail and "Andanson" comes up 65 times during that final summation.

This is another Power construct.

It is interesting that in his later reference to this (p210), Power feels free to change his "quoted" wording from "inappropriate to" to "nothing to do with".

Mishcon Note

129.   **Author**

Power: "The 'Mishcon Note' ... was a note that <u>Diana wrote</u> to her lawyer, Lord Mishcon ... with the express instruction it was to be handed to the police should the need arise" – p47

"<u>Diana's letter</u> to Lord Mishcon where she stated ... Charles intended having her murdered" – p100

"[Diana] described ... her husband's intentions to murder her ... in writing and [gave] this to her lawyer, Lord Mishcon" – p101

"The Mishcon Note (<u>Diana's note</u> to her lawyer in which she stated that her husband intended killing her)" – p109

"[Diana] gave [Mishcon] this note on 30th October 1995" – p113

"In 1995 (when Diana wrote the [Mishcon] note)" – p115

"Two notes from Diana via Mishcon and Burrell ... entered the public domain" – p115

"Diana took the [Mishcon] note to Lord Mishcon" – p118

"Mishcon would still have been reluctant to permit the disclosure of <u>Diana's note</u>" – p119

"Mishcon was entrusted with the safe keeping of <u>Diana's note</u>" – p119

"Diana took the trouble to write this note and give it to Lord Mishcon" – p119

"Diana ... unambiguously asked Lord Mishcon to keep this note secluded, but to reveal it should anything happen to her; this was the reason she gave the note to him" – p119

"The 'Mishcon Note' – so-named because Diana gave it to her lawyer Lord Mishcon" – p251

"The British police had a letter handed to them, written by Diana ... and given to her lawyer, Lord Mishcon" – p285

ALAN POWER EXPOSED

The Evidence and Comment: Princess Diana met with her lawyer, Lord Victor Mishcon, on 30 October 1995. The following morning Mishcon wrote up a note detailing comments made by Diana during the meeting – an excerpt where Mishcon reveals he is author appears below.

Power has falsely claimed 14 times throughout the book that it was Princess Diana that wrote this note and handed it to Mishcon at the meeting.

Using this claim as a foundation, Power then added a couple more fabrications:

a) That Diana gave an "express instruction [the note] was to be handed to the police should the need arise"

b) That the note named her husband Charles as the perpetrator of a crash plot (see below).

In a strange twist, at times Power actually changes the name of the note from the Mishcon Note to "Diana's note" – p119. Then later he explains that the "Mishcon Note" was "so-named because Diana gave it to ... Mishcon".

It is significant that Power quotes a short portion of the note – in the excerpt Mishcon reveals he is author of the note: page 113: "Because of the serious statements made by HRH [Diana] in the course of this [30 October 1995] meeting I decided unusually to write this entry and to give instructions that it should be securely held."

Power also talks on page 117 about Mishcon "[taking] steps to record his client's [Diana's] concern" and describes the note as Mishcon's "own note".

This raises the question: Is this a genuine mistake? If it is it raises serious doubts over whether Power scrutinised the inquest documents as thoroughly as he claims.

If it is a deliberate "error" then that raises an even more serious question: Why?

MISHCON NOTE

130.   **Content**

Power: "Diana's letter to Lord Mishcon where she stated ... <u>Charles</u> intended having her murdered" – p100

"[Diana] described ... <u>her husband's</u> intentions to murder her ... in writing and [gave] this to her lawyer, Lord Mishcon" – p101

"The Mishcon Note (Diana's note to her lawyer in which she stated that <u>her husband</u> intended killing her)" – p109

"The 'Mishcon Note' ... in which [Diana] described <u>her husband's</u> intention to kill her in a car 'accident'" – p251

"The letter [Mishcon Note] expressed fears that <u>her husband</u> was planning to kill her in a car crash" – p285

The Evidence: Inquest Transcripts, 15 Jan 08: 4.13:

Mishcon Note: "HRH said that ... efforts would be made if not to get rid of her (be it by some accident in her car such as pre-prepared brake failure or whatever)".

Comment: The Mishcon note makes no mention of who the perpetrator(s) of the attempted assassination of Diana would be.

Power has falsely claimed that Diana's husband Charles was named in the lawyer's document.

131.   **Time suppressed**

Power: "The police withheld [the Mishcon Note] for eight years, from both the French authorities and the English coroner" – p47

The Evidence and Comment: The Mishcon Note was received by the police on 18 September 1997 and was disclosed to the British coroner on 22 December 2003.

So it was withheld by the police for just over 6 years and 3 months. Power admits in other areas of his book that the suppression was for six years – but he has falsely stated here that it was for eight years.

132.   **MPS-Mishcon discussions**

Power: "[MPS Commissioner] Stevens was ... asked why they didn't give the [Mishcon] note to the French and the British coroners,

requesting them to ... keep its contents confidential from the public....
Stevens replied: 'No one did it – it was not done at that stage'. The
truth is that it wasn't done at any stage" – p122

The Evidence: Inquest transcripts, 14 Feb 08: 40.23:

Mansfield (Lawyer): "Did anyone explain to Lord Mishcon at any
stage, 'Look, we can overcome the confidentiality because there is a
duty to disclose because we can ask the Coroner to redact the parts of
the Mishcon note that may not have direct relevance or that may cause
pain'? ... That was all utterly possible, wasn't it?"

John Stevens (MPS Commissioner): "No one did it. It was not done at
that stage."

Comment: This question from Michael Mansfield was regarding
conversations between the police and Mishcon.

Power has twisted this, turning it into a question about "why [the
police] didn't give the [Mishcon] note to the French and the British
coroners", while requesting its contents remain confidential.

133. Timing of disclosure

Power: "[In 2003] Lord Mishcon went to the police concerning the
[Mishcon] note.... Within days this forced the subsequent disclosure of
the 'Mishcon Note'" – p73

The Evidence: Inquest transcripts, 14 Feb 08: 43.21:

Richard Horwell (Police Lawyer): "Mr Hodges [police officer] took
the Mishcon note to the Coroner on 22nd December 2003."

Comment: The Mishcon Note was disclosed on 22 December 2003 –
so nearly two months after Mishcon visited the police on October 30th.
Power has misled the reader by saying the Mishcon Note was
disclosed "within days" of Mishcon's visit.

134. Disclosure to media

Power: "The Mishcon Note appeared in the press on 23rd October
2003" – p113

"Both Burrell's and Mishcon's [notes] ... appeared in the press on 23rd
October [2003]" – p122

The Evidence and Comment: The first full disclosure of the Mishcon Note to the media occurred at the inquest on 15 January 2008. Prior to that there was a partial disclosure in the Paget Report, published on 14 December 2006.

Power has falsely claimed that the Mishcon Note was released to the press in 2003.

135. Timing of post-Burrell Note contact

Power: "Paul Burrell released a note [from Diana] to the press.... The next day ... Lord Mishcon went to the police concerning the note that he had given them six years earlier" – p73

"Burrell released the note to the press on 20th October 2003 and the next day Lord Mishcon telephoned the police" – p113

"Mishcon visited the police on 21st October [2003]" – p122

The Evidence: Inquest transcripts, 14 Feb 08: 42.9:

Mansfield (Lawyer) – referring to a document, probably Mishcon's police statement: "Mishcon is really very concerned about this note/letter or his note of the meeting being disclosed? He rings on 27th October."

John Stevens: "Yes."

Mansfield: "You are not available. He rings on the 29th, you are not available. He then sees you on the 30th,"

Comment: The Burrell Note was published on 20 October 2003 and Mishcon phoned Stevens a week later on the 27th, but they don't actually meet until the 30th of October.

Power has falsely stated that "Mishcon visited the police on 21st October" – nine days earlier than the meeting took place.

136. Lord Mishcon death – Timing & cause

Power: "Lord Mishcon ... died just before the inquest, on 28th January 2006 from a heart attack" – p119

The Evidence and Comment: This line appears to be wrong on three counts:

ALAN POWER EXPOSED

a) Lord Mishcon died on 27 January 2006 – not the 28th
b) Power says this was "just before" the inquest – the inquest started on 2 October 2007 – so there was a gap of 20 months between Mishcon's death and the inquest commencement
c) Power says Mishcon's death was from a "heart attack". The evidence from the time was that Mishcon had suffered a lengthy and progressive illness. His son, Peter, said that "he had ... been declining for a long time."

Sources: Lord Mishcon Obituary in *The Independent*, 1 February 2006; Princess Diana's Ex-Lawyer Dies, BBC News, 28 January 2006

137.   **Burrell Note – Timing of disclosure**

Power: "Burrell's ... [note] appeared in the press on 23rd October" – p122

The Evidence and Comment: The Burrell Note was published in the *Mirror* on 20 October 2003.

Power actually stated this correctly just nine pages earlier: "Burrell released the note to the press on 20th October 2003" – p113.

Alan Power:

"We have seen on numerous occasions where the facts have been misinterpreted and false information recorded" – page 238

Police Investigations

138. French Investigation - Duration

Power: "In 1999 an eighteen-month French judicial investigation concluded...." – p43

The Evidence: The French investigation commenced immediately after the crash on 31 August 1997 and concluded on 3 September 1999.

Comment: The French investigation ran for just over two years – not Power's 18 months.

139. Dauzonne contact – Timing

Power: "Six days after the crash Georges and Sabine Douzonne came forward" to the French investigation – p211

The Evidence: Inquest Transcripts, 29 Oct 07: 27.21:

Georges Dauzonne: "On Monday morning [1 September 1997] I called the commissariat of the 8th arrondissement where my office is.... They gave me a number to call and I called that number.... They said, 'We have had a lot of calls, sir. No, it does not seem to be very relevant for us'.... On the 17th or 18th September ... I called the police again."

Comment: Georges Dauzonne contacted the police on the day following the crash, and called them the second time 2½ weeks later, on September 17 or 18.

Power has falsely claimed that the Dauzonnes came forward "six days after the crash".

140. Investigation evidence – Mrs Levistre

Power: "Valerie [Levistre] ... [said] that the police had ... written her [interview] words down incorrectly. She said, 'If you say <u>black</u>, they write down <u>white</u>'" – p208

The Evidence: Inquest Transcripts, 15 Oct 07: 149.3:

Mrs Levistre: "I did depositions, and when I said 'white', it was written 'black'".

Comment: Power – in a move possibly indicative of the whole book – has managed to swap Mrs Levistre's "black" for "white" and her "white" for "black".

In doing this, Power has done exactly what Mrs Levistre was accusing the police of.[a]

141. White Fiat Uno – The authorities

Power: "The authorities were forced into ... admitting there was a Fiat Uno and a collision – or collisions – between this car and the Mercedes" – p221

The Evidence and Comment: At no point have the authorities ever said there was more than one collision between the Fiat Uno and the Mercedes.

This is a Power construct.

142. White Fiat Uno – Parameters

Power: "It was confirmed that [crash debris found] was from the turbo model Fiat Uno made between May 1983 and September 1989" – p221

The Evidence: Paget Report, p714

"The Mercedes was in collision with a white Fiat Uno built between 1983 and 1989 and painted with either Bianco Corfu 224 paint or Bianco 210 paint."

Comment: There was no finding from the crash debris that the Fiat Uno which collided with the Mercedes was a "turbo model".

Power has falsely claimed that there was.

---

[a] Regarding the evidence from Gary Hunter that he saw a white Mercedes and a small dark vehicle, Power writes: "It is very probable the ... Mercedes was black, not white and that the ... smaller car was white and not black" – p221.

POLICE INVESTIGATIONS

143.   Mercedes S280 – French inspection

Power: "The [Mercedes S280] was taken away and no one [was] allowed to examine it until public disquiet forced a sojourn to the UK in 2004" – p55

The Evidence: Paget Report, p423:

"Capitaine Francis Bechet ... examined the [Mercedes S280] at Nord Garage, Boulevard MacDonald on 1 September 1997.... Jacques Hebrard, Gilles Poully and Serge Moreau ... [carried out] their examination in October 1998."

Comment: The Mercedes underwent at least two inspections in France – one the day following the crash, 1 September 1997, and a second in October 1998.

Power has falsely stated that the first examination was in the UK after the vehicle's transfer in 2004.

144.   Henri Paul – Drinks consumed: Scotchbrook

Power: "Scotchbrook ... confirmed that Paul had taken two drinks that night, <u>and no more</u>" – p32

"Scotchbrook ... wrote a ... note ... [that] included the statement: 'Operation Paget would be saying that [Henri] had consumed two alcoholic drinks on the night of the incident', <u>and no more</u>" – p126

"Scotchbrook ... had written a note saying that Henri Paul had <u>only</u> had two drinks and <u>no more</u>" – p152

"Scotchbrook ... said that Paul had <u>only</u> had two drinks that night" – p222

"We also remind you of ... Scotchbrook's comment ... that Henri Paul had had <u>only</u> 'a few drinks and <u>no more</u>'" – p260

The Evidence: Inquest Transcripts, 28 Jan 08: 86.6:

DI Jane Scotchbrook (MPS DI on Operation Paget): "Operation Paget would be saying that [Henri] had consumed two alcoholic drinks on the night of the incident."

ALAN POWER EXPOSED

Comment: Power has altered the wording of Scotchbrook's statement. He has added the words "only" and "no more" – this may appear subtle, but it changes the meaning of what Scotchbrook said.

Scotchbrook was basically saying that Paget knew of two drinks Henri had consumed – these were the two Ricards he drank in the Ritz's Bar Vendôme after 10 p.m.

That is the fact of the case – only two drinks can be proven. By adding the words "only" and "no more", Power is falsely indicating that Scotchbrook was claiming that it could be proven Henri had no more than two drinks.

On the information available, that is not the case.

The Inquest

145.   Police inquest testimony

Power: "The police were seen [by the inquest] after the Christmas break <u>in January</u>" – p76

The Evidence: 21 police officers were cross-examined – Thierry Clotteaux on 6 November 2007; Hubert Pourceau on 6 November; Anthony Read 6 to 8 November; Gary Head on 27 November; Jeffrey Rees on 17 December; Philip Stoneham on 18 December; Colin Trimming on 7 January 2008; David Veness on 15 January; Paul Condon on 16-17 January; Roger Milburn on 28 January; David Davies on 31 January; Mark Monot on 4 February; Eric Gigou on 4 February and 10 March; Paul Laffan on 5 February; Jean-Claude Mulès on 5 February; Philip Easton on 7 and 19 February and 18 March; John Stevens on 14 February; David Meynell on 4 March; Mark Stokes on 6 and 12 March; Mark Hodges on 13 March; Vincent Delbreilh on 17 March.

Comment: Power states that the police were cross-examined in January 2008.

The evidence shows that out of the 21 officers only 5 were cross-examined in January – the remaining 16 were spread between November and December 2007 and February and March 2008. There were actually more police cross-examinations in February than January.

It is basic errors like this that reveal Power's analysis of the inquest was nowhere near as exhaustive as he claims – "I have personally scrutinised over four million words of [inquest] evidence" (p188).

146.   Attendance – French doctors

Power: "The court said that ... some witnesses ... need not attend but could offer affidavit evidence instead.... Most of these witnesses ...

ALAN POWER EXPOSED

would have made it impossible to render any verdict other than murder if they had attended.... These include ... all the French doctors" – p212

The Evidence and Comment: Power here indicates that none of the French doctors attended the inquest.

The following French doctors were cross-examined (with attendance dates):

Dr Arnaud Derossi – 11 December 2007

Dr Marc Lejay – 29 November 2007

Dr Frédéric Mailliez – 13 November 2007

Dr Jean-Marc Martino – 24 January 2008

Dr Bruno Riou – 15 November 2007

Prof Alain Pavie – 15 November 2007

147. Souad's attendance

Power: "Souad [Moufakkir] didn't attend court" – pxii (in Contents section)

The Evidence: Souad was cross-examined on 6 November 2007.

Comment: Souad Moufakkir attended court as a key witness to events in the Alma Tunnel – the white Fiat Uno and the bright flash.

148. Dauzonnes' attendance

Power: "Georges and Sabine Dauzonne ... didn't attend court" – pxiii (in Contents section)

The Evidence: Georges and Sabine Dauzonne were both cross-examined in court – Sabine on 29 October and Georges on 29 and 30 October 2007.

Comment: The Dauzonnes were the sole witnesses to the white Fiat Uno post-crash.

149. Alain Remy – Non-attendance

Power: "Alain Remy ... wasn't asked to attend court" – pxiii (Contents section)

"The very important witness, Alain Remy, whose offer to attend the hearing was declined" – p263

The Evidence: Summing Up: 1 Apr 08: 113.12:

THE INQUEST

Coroner: "Alain Remy's evidence was read to you [the jury] because we could not secure his attendance. Accordingly, he could not be cross-examined."

Comment: Baker's account indicates there was an attempt by the inquest to secure Remy's attendance. In support of this, Remy's statements were not read out until 18 March 2008, the last day for witness testimony.

Power provides no substantiation for his statement that Remy's "offer to attend the hearing was declined".

Earlier it was shown that Remy apparently didn't witness the Mercedes. There is a possibility that Remy didn't attend because he may have felt that his evidence wouldn't have come across well in court.

150.   **Video link evidence**

Power: "Video links do not permit the jury sight of a witness's response to the questions asked by lawyers" – p76

The Evidence and Comment: Although I didn't attend the inquest I do have input from a journalist who did attend every day of the hearings.

He and another person, who attended court on some of the days the video link was set up, have both confirmed that the jury could see the witness in Paris right through their period of testimony. The camera focused on the witness the whole time – even when questions were being put by the lawyers.

This raises the question: Did Alan Power – who says his investigation started five years before the inquest – actually attend the inquest at all, or receive input from anyone who attended?

ALAN POWER EXPOSED

151.   Evidence from paparazzi

Power: "None of [the paparazzi] attended court and few even gave affidavit evidence" – p234

The Evidence: There were ten paparazzi in the Alma Tunnel following the crash. All of them provided statements that were read out at the inquest – the details including number of statements and dates read out are below.

Serge Arnal – 4 statements – 12 March 2008

Nikola Arsov – 4 statements – 11 March 2008

Serge Benhamou – 3 statements – 10 March 2008

Fabrice Chassery – 3 statements – 13 March 2008

Alain Guizard – 3 statements – 10 March 2008

Jacques Langevin – 5 statements – 12 March 2008

Christian Martinez – 4 statements – 10 March 2008

David Odekerken – 5 statements – 11 March 2008

Romuald Rat – 4 statements – 11 March 2008

Laslo Veres – 3 statements – 11 March 2008

Comment: All the paparazzi who were present in the Alma Tunnel following the crash had their police statements read out at the inquest. Power has lied when he states that only a few gave evidence.

152.   MI6 evidence in court

Power: "MI6 [personnel] ... displayed a nervous disposition in court and were clearly not enjoying their exposure" – p95

The Evidence: Inquest Transcripts, 20 Feb 08: 1.7:

Coroner: "In order to protect the identities of those [MI6 personnel] giving evidence, they will be identified by letters or numbers, rather than their names, and their physical appearance will be concealed.... The only people permitted in this room will be the jury, court officials, the interested persons and their respective solicitors and counsel."

Comment: The media and public were prevented from viewing all but one of the MI6 personnel who gave evidence.

Power fails to explain how he was able to establish that they "displayed a nervous disposition in court".

THE INQUEST

153.   **Jury verdict**

Power: "The inquiry [was] wound up following the completion of the inquests in April 2008. Its conclusions were emphatic.... All the evidence pointed towards a tragic accident caused by Henri Paul, but exacerbated by the actions of the paparazzi. This is the end of the official story. Yet ... the questions refuse to go away. Let us now look at the alternative version of events" – p43

The Evidence: Inquest transcripts, 7 Apr 08: 5.5:

Jury Foreman: "The verdict is unlawful killing, grossly negligent driving of the following vehicles and of the Mercedes."

Comment: Power discusses verdicts at length in his book – he mentions the word "verdict" 68 times and the term "unlawful killing" 18 times. Yet at no point does he clearly state what the inquest jury's verdict was.

The above quote – from page 43 – appears to merge the Paget investigation with the inquest. But Power here clearly states that "the end of the official story" is "a tragic accident caused by Henri Paul, but exacerbated by the actions of the paparazzi".

This neither matches the jury's verdict nor the Paget finding. Paget found that it was an accident caused by Henri Paul but Stevens made no declaration regarding paparazzi involvement.

Then the inquest jury found unlawful killing by the Mercedes and following vehicles – see above.

"The end of the official story" was the inquest verdict – so it is logical to presume that is what Power is referring to. This logic is supported by Power's failure to state the jury's verdict throughout the remainder of the book.

When one considers that this book is about the inquest, this is an extraordinary flaw – that Power fails to correctly state the inquest jury's verdict.

ALAN POWER EXPOSED

154. **Unlawful killing by following vehicles**

Power: "There was no excuse for forbidding a verdict of 'unlawful killing by persons unknown'" – p68

"An 'unlawful killing by persons unknown' verdict ... [was] denied by ... Baker" – p70

"Baker ... said ... that the jury were not permitted to find for unlawful killing by persons unknown" – p157

"[It was] not acceptable to permit an 'unlawful killing by persons unknown' verdict" – p157

"To not permit the jury a verdict option of 'unlawful killing by persons unknown' is an abuse of justice, pure and simple" – p158

"[An] 'unlawful killing by persons unknown' [verdict] ... would have been a de facto conviction of MI6 and extremely dangerous for the monarchy" – p188

"How could the ... jury [be] denied a verdict of unlawful killing by persons unknown if justice was being sought?" – p214

"The option for 'unlawful killing by persons unknown' had been excluded from the jury" – p231

"Baker ... says in his summation that he can't permit the jury the option of finding for unlawful killing by persons unknown because he couldn't be sure there was sufficient evidence" – p240

"Baker wasn't prepared to permit the jury the option of doing their democratic duty by finding for unlawful killing by persons unknown" – p261

"It's unacceptable to find for unlawful killing by persons unknown because the coroner couldn't be sure that these aggressive, loitering, hindering and blocking vehicles were assassins" – p262

"These two jurors [who dissented] were probably not the only ones who would have opted for a verdict of unlawful killing by persons unknown if they had had the option" – p262

"Since the jury were not permitted the option of the verdict 'unlawful killing by persons unknown' they were effectively prevented from returning any verdict that could cause a serious problem to the state and the monarchy" – p274

THE INQUEST

The Evidence: Summing Up: 31 Mar 08: 11.25:

Coroner: "Applying the law, I have determined that it is not open to you to find that this was unlawful killing by the Duke of Edinburgh or anyone else in a staged accident."

Summing Up: 31 Mar 08: 13.25:

Coroner: "My direction in law to you is, as I have said, that it is not open to you to find that Diana and Dodi were unlawfully killed in a staged accident."

Comment: Baker told the jury that there would be no verdict option for "unlawful killing ... in a staged accident", otherwise known as murder.

Power has turned this into: "Baker ... says ... that he can't permit ... the option of ... unlawful killing by persons unknown" (p240). That option is not the equivalent of murder – it can be murder, but it also can be manslaughter.

As it turned out the final jury verdict – and allowed by Baker – included unlawful killing by following vehicles – this is the equivalent of unlawful killing by persons unknown. The persons on or in the following vehicles were unidentified – they were effectively "persons unknown".

The introduction of the term "unlawful killing by persons unknown" is actually a Power construct – it does not appear once in the 117 pages of lawyer-coroner debate over possible verdicts that took place, without the jury present, on 20 March 2008.

It is significant that Power mentions "unlawful killing by persons unknown" 13 times in his book – stating it was not a verdict option – but makes no mention at all of the actual jury verdict – see above – of unlawful killing by following vehicles.

155.   Dissenting jurors

Power: "These two jurors [who dissented] were probably not the only ones who would have opted for a verdict of unlawful killing by persons unknown if they had had the option" – p262

ALAN POWER EXPOSED

The Evidence: Inquest transcripts, 7 Apr 08: 5.11:
Coroner: "How many agreed and how many dissented?"
Jury Foreman: "Nine, sir.... The deceased is Diana, Princess of Wales.... The crash was caused or contributed to by the speed and manner of driving of the Mercedes, the speed and manner of driving of the following vehicles, the impairment of the judgment of the driver of the Mercedes through alcohol. Nine of us are agreed on those points, sir. In addition, the death of the deceased was caused or contributed to by the fact that the deceased was not wearing a seat-belt, the fact that the Mercedes struck the pillar in the Alma Tunnel, rather than colliding with something else, and we are unanimously agreed on that."
Comment: Power has stated that the two dissenting jurors "would have opted for a verdict of unlawful killing by persons unknown if they had had the option".
It is impossible to know what the dissenting jurors thought – they could have wanted a murder verdict, or they could have wanted an accidental death verdict.

156.　　　Inquest conclusion

Power: "The inquests ... ended with the coroner's summation on 2nd April 2008" – p74
The Evidence and Comment: The inquests concluded with the jury's verdict – not the summation – on 7th April 2008, five days later than Power states.

157.　　　Inquest transcripts – Size

Power: "I have personally scrutinised over four million words of evidence produced over a six month period during and after the inquests" – p188
The Evidence and Comment: There are 7,391 pages of inquest transcripts with an average of around 357 words per page. This makes in total approximately 2.64 million words in the entire inquest – that is substantially less than the 4 million words of inquest evidence Power claims to have scrutinised.

Other Issues

158.   Ritz Hotel – Location

Power: "Rue de Rivoli, where the [Ritz] hotel's rear exit is located" – p223

The Evidence and Comment: The rear exit of the Ritz Hotel is on Rue Cambon.

Power wrongly states it is on Rue de Rivoli, which is about 300 metres from the Ritz.

159.   Michelle Blanchard – Laurent Relationship

Power: "This was further confirmed by Michelle [Blanchard], David's mother" – p198

The Evidence: Inquest transcripts, 11 Oct 07: 23.5:

David Laurent: "In the car with me [was] ... my mother-in-law, Michelle Blanchard".

Comment: At the time of the crash Michelle was the mother of Laurent's girlfriend, Nathalie. By the time Laurent gave his evidence, he had married Nathalie and Michelle became his mother-in-law. Michelle Blanchard is not David Laurent's mother, as stated by Power.

160.   Gary Hunter's death

Power: "Gary Hunter ... died just months before the Inquest" – pxiii (in Contents section)

The Evidence: Paget Report, p494:

"Gary Hunter died in February 2004".

Comment: Power states that Hunter died "just months before the inquest" – the reality is he died 3 years and 8 months before the inquest.

161. Rees-Jones' book

Power: "Rees-Jones and Wingfield employed a ghost-writer to write ... *The Bodyguard's Story*" – p137

The Evidence and Comment: Moira Johnston was the writer of the Rees-Jones book. There is no evidence that Wingfield was involved with the writing of the book – it is essentially Rees-Jones' story, written "with Moira Johnston". Wingfield was clearly interviewed by Johnston.

In the Preface to the book Rees-Jones makes a "statement" and says: "This book is my story" – pxii, *The Bodyguard's Story*.

162. Karen MacKenzie – Occupation

Power: "Mrs Karen Mackenzie, an office worker at Al Fayed's security offices in Park Lane" – p174

The Evidence: Inquest Transcripts, 11 Feb 08: 60.7:

Hough (Lawyer): "You were housekeeper at the Al Fayed family residence at 60 Park Lane; is that right?"

Karen MacKenzie (Al Fayed housekeeper): "That is correct."

Hough: "In that capacity, you were responsible for a number of domestic staff?"

MacKenzie: "Yes."

Comment: Karen MacKenzie was an Al Fayed housekeeper – Power has wrongly stated she was an office worker.

163. Landmines dossier – Size

Power: "Simmons said she placed the inch-thick dossier ... under her mattress" – p183

The Evidence: Inquest Transcripts, 10 Jan 08: 74.3:

Simone Simmons (Friend of Diana): "[The landmines dossier] was a file that started off little and ... it just grew and grew and grew (indicates)."

....Mansfield (Lawyer): "Is it about 6 inches deep; is that fair?"

Simmons: "It started off really little, like a quarter of an inch and it grew to about ... 4 to 6 inches.... It was very big."

OTHER ISSUES

Comment: The dossier was approximately five inches thick – Power has falsely described it as an "inch-thick".

164.   Nicholas Soames – Relationship to Churchill

Power: "Nicholas Soames [is] the <u>great-grandson</u> of Sir Winston Churchill" – p183

The Evidence and Comment: Soames is the <u>grandson</u> of Churchill – not the great-grandson.

165.   Nicholas Soames – Newsnight

Power: "Soames ... appeared ... on BBC television in support of Prince Charles ... on *Newsweek*" – p184

The Evidence: Inquest Transcripts, 12 Dec 07: 60.25:

Mansfield (Lawyer): "On *Newsnight* ... you went on to describe [Diana] in particularly vitriolic terms.... The way you put it was this: 'It really is the advanced stages of paranoia.' That is how you put it, wasn't it?"

Nicholas Soames (Minister for Armed Forces): "It was."

Comment: Soames appeared on *Newsnight* – not "Newsweek" as stated by Power.

166.   L'Hostis' statement

Power: "Asked about a witness statement she was supposed to have signed at 2.20am, two hours after the attack, L'Hostis said that it wasn't her signature and not her statement" – pp196-7

The Evidence: Inquest Transcripts, 24 Oct 07: 83.1:

Croxford (Lawyer): "The first witness statement that you made at 20 past two in the morning.... Do you recognise the handwriting?"

L'Hostis: "No."

Croxford: "It is not yours?"

L'Hostis: "It is not mine."

Comment: L'Hostis was asked if it was her handwriting and says it wasn't.

153

This was not pursued by the lawyers present – it may be that the statement was handwritten by a French police officer and then read through and signed by L'Hostis.

Power has changed this to: "it wasn't her signature and not her statement". This is a complete misrepresentation and twisting of what L'Hostis said – the signature was not discussed in court and L'Hostis never said it wasn't her statement.

I suggest that if the signature had not been hers then she would have said that. This 2.20 a.m. statement was quoted to L'Hostis in court and she never queried the content of it.

167. Paul Burrell – Occupation

Power: "Before becoming <u>footman</u> to Charles, Prince of Wales, Paul Burrell did the same job for Queen Elizabeth" – p178

The Evidence: Inquest Transcripts, 14 Jan 08: 7.23:

Burnett (Lawyer): "In 1987, did you leave the personal service of Her Majesty and go to work as <u>butler</u> for the Prince and Princess of Wales at Highgrove?"

Paul Burrell (Diana's butler): "Yes, I did."

Comment: Burrell worked as butler for both Charles and Diana – he never was "footman to Charles" as Power has falsely claimed.

168. Death of Queen Astrid

Power: "Place de la Reine Astrid [near the Alma Tunnel] ... ironically is named after a Belgian queen who died here in a car accident" – p202

The Evidence and Comment: Queen Astrid of Belgium died in a car accident at Kussnacht, Switzerland on 29 August 1935, aged 29. *Time* magazine ran the story on 9 September 1935, "Belgium: Death of Astrid".

Power has taken the death of Astrid in Switzerland and falsely transferred it to a location near the Alma Tunnel, apparently to make interesting reading – but in the process, Power lies to his readers.

Word Manipulation

169.   "Uncontroversial" – "Incontrovertible"

At the inquest witness evidence was described as <u>uncontroversial</u> if it was not disputed by any of the interested parties.

Power states that Scott Baker said: "Where evidence is <u>incontrovertible</u> it makes sense to read the evidence rather than bring the witness to court" (p247).

Power fails to reference this and it is simply not a statement Baker made.

Baker did however indicate that if a witness' evidence was <u>uncontroversial</u> then a statement would be read out, rather than bringing the witness to court. Referring for example to the evidence of Grigori Rassinier, Baker said: "The reason that this witness has not been called to give evidence is that his evidence has been agreed to be <u>uncontroversial</u> and can be read to you rather than troubling him to come to court."

There is a huge difference in meaning between "incontrovertible" and "uncontroversial".

"Uncontroversial" means the evidence was accepted by the interested parties – in other words, the lawyers felt they did not need to subject the witness to cross-examination to test their evidence.

"Incontrovertible" evidence was evidence that couldn't be contested because of its certainty. At the inquest certain CCTV footage was deemed to be incontrovertible, as was the forensic evidence of a collision between the Mercedes and a white Fiat Uno.

Power falsely stated that the evidence of Grigori Rassinier (pp212, 213), Elizabeth Dion (pp215, 216, 247) and Didier Gamblin (p247) was all incontrovertible.

Power then took this a step further and stated: "All incontrovertible evidence, such as Gamblin, Dr Dion and other eyewitnesses, was evidence that collectively could bring the curtain down [on the monarchy]" (p247).

The reality is that it would be extremely unusual for the evidence of a witness to be deemed as incontrovertible – not contestable – particularly in a courtroom.

Problems with Names

There is a theme of misspelling or misrepresenting names – primarily people's names – throughout this book. This is surprising, coming from an author who promotes himself as an investigator and researcher and says he has "personally scrutinised" the entire 7,000 pages of inquest transcripts (p188).

170.   **Lord Justice Scott Baker** – Inquest coroner
Scott Baker is mentioned 159 times in the book.
There are several problems:
- Power incorrectly calls him "<u>Lord</u> Scott Baker" 8 times – example on p69
- on one occasion Baker's name is incorrectly hyphenated as "Scott-Baker" – p69
- on one occasion Power incorrectly calls him "Lord <u>Robert</u> Scott Baker" – p74
- on one occasion Power incorrectly calls him "<u>Mr Justice</u> Scott Baker" – p74

171.   **Dodi Fayed** – Died in the crash, Diana's lover
Dodi's official first name is "Emad" – Power misspelt this as "Ema<u>u</u>d" both times he used it – p3 and p297 (in the Index).

172.   **Trevor Rees-Jones** – Bodyguard
Rees-Jones appears 48 times in the book. He is wrongly referred to as "Trevor Jones" three times (e.g. p137) and on 24 occasions Rees-Jones is not hyphenated – incorrectly shown as "Rees Jones" (e.g. p176).

ALAN POWER EXPOSED

At two points in the book Power states that Rees-Jones is "now Trevor Jones" (pp137, 172) – that is false. At the inquest Rees-Jones was known as "Trevor Rees".

173.   **Georges & Sabine Dauzonne** – Fiat Uno witnesses
The Dauzonnes are mentioned five times and all are misspelt as "Douzonne" – examples are pxiii (in the Contents) and p211.

174.   **Martyn Gregory** – Prominent accident theorist
Power misspells Gregory's first name as "Martin" – pxv (in Acknowledgements section).

175.   **Kez Wingfield** – Bodyguard
Wingfield is mentioned 30 times – the first two instances are misspelt as "Winfield" – pp32 and 33.

176.   **Nathalie Blanchard** – Witness in Alma Tunnel
Nathalie appears twice in the book – both mentions on page 197. The first is spelt correctly and the second is misspelt as "Natalie".

177.   **Sandra Davis** – Lawyer representing Diana
Sandra Davis is mentioned just once – her surname is misspelt as "Davies" – p113

178.   **John Stevens** – MPS Commissioner
John Stevens appears in the book 67 times – of those, his surname is misspelt 6 times as "Stephens" – example p252

179.   **Sarah McCorquodale** – Diana's sister
Sarah McCorquodale appears 3 times in the book – on all occasions her surname is misspelt as McCorqodale – example p289

PROBLEMS WITH NAMES

180. **Dominique Lecomte** – French pathologist
Dominique Lecomte appears 13 times in the book – in all cases her surname is misspelt as "Lecompte" – example p57

181. **François Levistre** – Eye-witness in Alma Tunnel
Levistre's full name occurs 9 times in the book – on two occasions his first name as misspelt as "Françoise" – on p58 and p297 (Index)

182. **Brian Anderson** – Eye-witness before Alma Tunnel
Brian Anderson is mentioned 22 times in the book – of those, his surname is misspelt 20 times as "Andersen" – example on pxiii (Contents section). In the other two instances his name is spelt correctly.

183. **Olivier Partouche** – Eye-witness near tunnel
Olivier Partouche appears 16 times in the book. On one occasion (p201) his first name is misspelt as "Oliver".

184. **Elisabeth Andanson** – wife of James Andanson
Elisabeth Andanson appears 26 times through the book – in all cases her first name is misspelt as "Elizabeth" – example on p62.

185. **James Gilbey** – friend of Diana
James Gilbey appears three times and each time his surname is misspelt as "Gilby", example p95.

186. **Michael Messinger** – MPS Commander
Michael Messinger appears five times – each time his surname is misspelt as "Messenger", example p130.

ALAN POWER EXPOSED

187.   **Martine Monteil** – Head of Brigade Criminelle
Martine Monteil is mentioned nine times in the book. On two occasions Power misspelt her surname as "Comiele" – both on page 132.

188.   **John Macnamara** – Harrods Head of Security
John Macnamara appears 77 times – on two occasions his surname is misspelt as "McNamara" – e.g. p138.

189.   **Souad Moufakkir** – Key eye-witness in tunnel
Moufakkir is mentioned 17 times in the book – her surname is spelt correctly once (pxii in the Contents) and the remaining 16 mentions are misspelt "Mouffakir" (e.g. p199).

190.   **Mohammed Medjahdi** – boyfriend of Souad
Medjahdi is mentioned nine times – in the first instance both his first and surnames are spelt incorrectly: "Mohamed Mejhadi" (pxii in the Contents).
The remaining eight mentions the first name is correct, but the surname, although spelt differently – "Medjhadi" – is still incorrect.

191.   **Alberto Repossi** – Engagement ring jeweller
Alberto Repossi appears five times – on one occasion his first name is misspelt as "Albert" – p138.

192.   **Françoise Dard** – wife of friend of James Andanson
Françoise Dard appears three times – on one occasion her first name is misspelt as "François" – p159.
On p168 Power refers to "Mrs Joséphine Dard" – the context indicates he is actually meaning Mrs Françoise Dard.

193.   **Gerald Posner** – US journalist
Gerald Posner appears six times – every time his surname is misspelt as "Postner" – e.g. p139.

PROBLEMS WITH NAMES

194. **JoAnn Grube** – NSA Deputy Director of Policy
JoAnn Grube appears just once – her surname is misspelt as "Grub<u>b</u>" –
p139.
Power also gets her position wrong – he states she is "director of
policy", whereas she actually is "deputy director of policy" – Inquest
Transcripts, 13 Mar 08: 81.15.

195. **Vincent L'Hotellier** – Head Barman, Ritz Hotel
Vincent L'Hotellier appears twice – both times his surname is misspelt
as "l'<u>O</u>te<u>l</u>ier" – both on p143.

196. **Aotal** - Drug that reduces desire for alcohol
Power mentions Aotal twice – on both occasions it is misspelt as
"A<u>y</u>otal" – e.g. p152.

197. **Avenue des Champs-Elysées** – Paris street
Avenue des Champs-Elysées only appears once – it is misspelt as
"Avenue <u>de</u> Champs-Elysées" – p206

198. **Jonikal** – the yacht Diana and Dodi cruised on
The *Jonikal* is mentioned seven times and all are misspelt as "Joni<u>c</u>al"
– examples are p4 and p6.

199. **Brigade Criminelle** – French police department
The Brigade Criminelle appears four times. Power calls it the
"Criminal Brigade" twice (pp48, 198), the "Criminale brigade" once
(p55) and finally the "Brigade Criminale" (p132). All are incorrect.

200. **Dis-Moi-Oui** – Diana-Dodi engagement ring range
This appears once and Power misspelt it as "Di<u>te</u>s-moi-oui" – p5

161

ALAN POWER EXPOSED

201.   **Montpellier** – city in the South of France
Montpellier appears three times – each time it is misspelt as
"Montpelier" – e.g. p210

The SAS Factor

Alan Power makes a bold promise on page 1 of *The Princess Diana Conspiracy*: "Herein I shall expound significant evidence that Diana's death was an assassination by 'The Increment', an SAS/SBS military attachment to ... MI6".

Power continues: "Beginning in November 2003 I decided to review this [SAS/SBS] evidence and, in search of the truth, I began on a long, instructive but perilous journey. Ten years later, greatly assisted by evidence from the official inquests, I believe that the truth of what happened on that fateful night in Paris is now uncovered; evidence that would satisfy any honest court in the world."

This effectively is Power's overall outline of the book – he will publicise "significant evidence" that the Special Forces carried out the assassination of Princess Diana. He says that with both that evidence and the inquest evidence, he has finally arrived at the truth of what occurred.

This sounds good and the reader is then expecting the book to contain significant new evidence of SAS/SBS involvement in the assassination.

It doesn't.

Power profoundly fails to deliver on his promise of revealing significant new evidence, or indeed any new evidence, of SAS involvement.

Instead what Power serves up is a rehash of what the inquest heard and Richard Tomlinson has said, but written from Power's perspective – with his associated exaggeration, fantasy and manipulation of evidence.

The question is: Why does Power make this false claim that he will "expound significant evidence" of Special Forces involvement?

ALAN POWER EXPOSED

And a second question is: Why does he make it the premise of his book?

To understand more about this one needs to study the timing of the publicity and publication of *The Princess Diana Conspiracy*.

The book was scheduled months in advance for release on 29 August 2013 – just two days ahead of the 16th anniversary of the death of Princess Diana.

On Saturday night 17 August 2013 Scotland Yard announced it was "scoping information in relation to the deaths" of Diana and Dodi and "assessing its relevance and credibility". The information related to a letter written by the mother-in-law of a serving SAS soldier, known as Soldier N. She stated that her daughter had been told by her husband that "it was the SAS who arranged Princess Diana's death and that has been covered up". This was later confirmed by Soldier N's wife and step-father-in-law.

Within hours of this police announcement Power conducted his most prominent newspaper interview – this was with the *New York Post* and was published online at 4 a.m. NY time (10 a.m. in London) on August 18. In it Power said that he had conducted interviews with former SAS officers – this is something he failed to mention anywhere in his book. He went on to say that he had "no idea" his book would "hit print just as Scotland Yard was probing identical allegations" as he is raising himself.

Is this true – that Power was unaware of the Soldier N allegation before the Scotland Yard announcement?

Or in other words: Is it true that Power didn't have inside knowledge and a) his book's content was not influenced by the Soldier N allegation; and b) the book's timing of publication was not influenced by the timing of the MPS scoping announcement?

There is a significant point to consider.

During over 16 years since the death of Princess Diana there have been dozens of books written about the event. None of them have used SAS involvement as their basic premise. The possibility has been

THE SAS FACTOR

mentioned, but no book has focused on it in the way Power's has – using it as the book's premise.

Yet *The Princess Diana Conspiracy* is published within two weeks of a major police announcement relating to the first concrete evidence of SAS involvement in the assassination.

The question is: Is that an incredible coincidence?

The odds of this happening – the first Diana death book focusing on the SAS being published within two weeks of the first actual SAS-related evidence being publicised – are approximately 1 in 200.

So the coincidence is possible, but very unlikely.

It is already known that the British authorities were made aware of the Soldier N allegation at the time N's SAS Commander and the police received the mother-in-law's letter – that was in September 2011.

So the authorities had almost two years to ponder over how they would deal with the allegation, before it reached the public domain in August 2013.

The result of this timing coincidence – Power's book being available within days of the police announcement – meant that the book created substantial interest and sold widely, particularly among the sections of the community that are open to accepting the possibility of the assassination of Diana. The reason this happened was primarily because Power was claiming his book matched the Soldier N evidence. And it is true that the premise of the book did.

Is there any possible scenario where the UK Establishment could benefit from a book such as Power's – a book that is laden with easily provable error but draws valid conclusions regarding the deaths – selling well within the conspiracy community?

There is one possibility.

If a book is widely read and believed and then at some future point it is shown to be full of errors and even fraudulent, then that could have the effect of not just destroying that book – it could do serious damage to the entire Diana conspiracy movement.

ALAN POWER EXPOSED

The point here is that it is not good enough that a book reaches the right conclusion – death at the hands of MI6 using the SAS, under the orders of senior royals. Of equal importance is how that conclusion is arrived at. If the route to the conclusion is replete with errors then the conclusion becomes worthless. Faulty reasoning – something Power's book is full of – has the power to destroy the whole book and take the conclusions with it.

My hope is that the publication of this book review – by a Diana conspiracy author, seen by others as an expert on the case – will limit the damage that could otherwise be caused by the exposure of the true nature of *The Princess Diana Conspiracy*.

In the process I seek to protect the Diana conspiracy – an assassination that can be proven and stands powerfully, without any requirement to manufacture evidence or manipulate the facts.

Questions Around Authorship

There are factors that raise the possibility *The Princess Diana Conspiracy* was not authored by Alan Power acting alone.
None of the following points on their own prove anything, but taken together it is possible they indicate Power is not the sole author.
The factors are:

    1) The variability of wording.

References to speed in mph differ – there is "[word] mph" (p198); "[word] miles per hour" (p223); "[numerals] mph" (p41).
References to speed in kph also differ – there is "[word] km/h" (p201); "[word] km per hour" (p212); "[numerals] km/hr" (p189).
Remy's description of the Mercedes' speed occurs three times and all are shown differently. On p41 – "87-94mph"; on p189 – "87/94km/hr"; on p214 – "eighty-seven to ninety-four km/h".
Distances are measured using "miles" ten times – e.g. p162 – and using "kilometres" at least five times – e.g. p63.
Then "metres" is used five times – e.g. p223 – and "yards" seven times – e.g. p218.

    2) The errors in names.[a]

A notable factor regarding the name problems is that outside of the proper nouns there are very few typos in the book – probably less than 10 in about 300 pages.
So a spell check has been done, but spell checks do not always correct proper nouns.
A close look at the naming errors – there are around 30 listed earlier – reveals two key points:

---

[a] See earlier section on Problems with Names.

ALAN POWER EXPOSED

a)   Many of the errors are not uniform throughout the book. For example, Wingfield is only misspelt twice out of 30 mentions; Stevens is misspelt six times out of 67 mentions.

b)   Many of the errors appear to be names that have been written according to their sound. Using the above two examples, Wingfield, if typed from a voice recording or dictation, could be easily shown as "Winfield", and the same applies to Stevens written as "Stephens". This is not the type of error we would see if this book had been written as a result of investigative research, as claimed by Power. An investigative author, by the time he or she finally gets to write the book after possibly years of research, is very familiar with seeing the written names of the key people. So they are most unlikely to spell them wrong – and certainly not to the level of error we see in Power's book. The nature of the misspelling of these proper nouns raises the possibility that sections of the book were typed by someone who was: a) unfamiliar with the names – i.e. not someone who had seen the names repeatedly during their research; and b) typing from a recording or dictation from another person.

3)   The acknowledgements.
Power fails to acknowledge the help of anyone in his "Acknowledgments". He lists books and newspapers but mentions no help.
This is extremely unusual for an investigative writer. Generally over the ten years – from 2003 to 2013 – there will be someone who has helped in some way.
Power mentions no one at all.
Why?

4)   Use of "we".
Throughout the book Power regularly uses the words "we" or "us" when referring to the author.
Examples are: "We believe it is now proven" – p27; "We show that MI6" – p68; "Our view that" – p121; "This doesn't alter our logic" – p145; "We now produce maps" – p188; "We also remind you" – p260;

QUESTIONS AROUND AUTHORSHIP

"We once more repeat" – p261; "We hope your verdict is building" – p271.

Why does Power use "we" and "us" if he is the sole author?

Some authors do use "we" or "us" to draw the reader in – I include myself – but it is the context that is significant with this: e.g. "We also remind you".

    5) Variation in content.

There are subjects addressed where the author's stance changes significantly in different areas of the book.

A graphic example is the handling of the Mishcon Note. For most of the book the author falsely treats it as a note written by Diana, yet on page 117 it is described as Mishcon's "own note".

As mentioned, these five factors raise the possibility of *The Princess Diana Conspiracy* being authored by more than one person.

Conclusion

On page 228 of *The Princess Diana Conspiracy*, under the heading "Rationalising the Evidence", Power addresses his readers: "You will discern the points that are proven [in this book] and, rest assured, my perception is not given to exaggeration or fancy but is based on the facts".

Unfortunately the opposite is the truth.

Alan Power's *The Princess Diana Conspiracy* is a mix of fiction, fact and fantasy – all rolled into one book that falsely purports to be the result of ten years of comprehensive investigative research.

The big question is: Why?

Why has Power produced a book that includes a tidal wave of error, but then out of all that emerges with a true conclusion of what occurred?

Is the book written by an amazingly incompetent author, who just happens to stumble into the truth when he draws his conclusions?

Or, is it the ramblings of a lazy, lying author who has simply twisted witness evidence to fit his own scenario of what occurred?

Or a third possibility – is Power's book part of a coordinated plot to eventually undermine the Diana conspiracy movement: the creation of a work that is so full of errors that it can in the future be easily debunked with possibly severe consequences for the conspiracy movement?

Which is it? A dishonest author, an incompetent writer, or a vicious plot?

Central to the answer could be the reality of the book's premise – SAS involvement – and the timing of publication – within a fortnight of the sensational revelations of SAS involvement. The timing became

ALAN POWER EXPOSED

central to the book's success. It was a sensation in itself that in the same timeframe as the police announcement, an author could emerge within hours with a ready to roll book – a book that promised to flesh out the exact same scenario as Scotland Yard was about to scope: SAS involvement.

Power himself stated on US TV seven days after the police scoping announcement that it was "a pure and amazing coincidence". He said it is "quite remarkable" and attributed it to "someone above looking down" and helping justice come about. He continued: "Soldier N ... just happens to mirror exactly what I'm saying in the book." [a]

As mentioned earlier, the odds of this occurring as a coincidence are around 1 in 200. Or put another way, there is approximately a 99.5% chance that it is not a coincidence.

The evidence in this book reveals that the reason for the Power errors is not simply pure incompetence. There are documented instances of Power deliberately altering witness accounts to fit with his own false scenario of what occurred.

This indicates that the first option of the above three – incompetent author – is not a possible explanation for all the errors in the book. That leaves dishonest writer or orchestrated plot.

I believe there is not enough evidence to conclusively determine either way, although I suggest there appears to be significantly more evidence pointing to a possible plot than not.

This evidence includes:

a) The possibility of more than one author – discussed earlier
b) The "pure and amazing coincidence" – Soldier N's allegations emerging 12 days ahead of the book's publication date – discussed earlier
c) The inclusion of the most vocal accident theorist in the UK, Martyn Gregory, in the list of books acknowledged – and the exclusion of any books that deal with the inquest, the major focus of Power's book

---

[a] Geraldo At Large, Fox News, 24 August 2013.

CONCLUSION

d) The scale of error in the book is so great that it makes it relatively easy to destroy its credibility – this may have been organised in advance for a future debunking

e) The two year delay, between the authorities becoming aware of N's allegation and the scoping announcement, certainly gave the Establishment plenty of time to work out a detailed strategy for dealing with it – Power could be part of that.

Conversely, there is also evidence that could point to Power acting alone as a dishonest author – no orchestrated plot:

a) *The Princess Diana Conspiracy* is self-published – wouldn't the Establishment employ a publisher?

b) The presentation of the book as an investigative work is extremely poor – there are no headers, no proper Bibliography, the maps and pictures inside are generally of little use or are unreadable (or both), the Index is inadequate and there are no Notes at all.

c) Power is very outspoken against the Establishment in the book and at times he does successfully reflect the position of the Diana conspiracy.

One could of course argue that the book would have to be anti-Establishment and include conspiracy arguments for readability by its target audience, primarily people who are open to the possibility of a Diana assassination. The self-publishing and the poor presentation has not appeared to affect the book's wide distribution – and possibly those factors act as a cover, after all military intelligence is used to providing covers.

So I can conclude that the evidence points to a possible conspiracy to help destroy the Diana conspiracy movement – but there is not enough evidence to provide any certainty.

Whatever the case though, the Power book, despite purporting to support and document the conspiracy, actually provides no help to it, because it is simply too full of error.

ALAN POWER EXPOSED

That is something that is provable and I believe this book review –
which documents hundreds of the errors and reveals some are
fraudulent – does show that.

It is my aim to protect the integrity and future of the Princess Diana
conspiracy – a conspiracy has I believe already been proven in other
books. It is my sincere hope that this book review helps to achieve
that.

Evidence, Maps, Diagrams & Photos

Figure 1 Excerpt from Diana and Charles' Certificate of Divorce 24
Figure 2 Receipt for engagement ring purchased by Dodi 30 August 1997 ..50
Figure 3 Thierry Hackett's diagram of Mercedes pursued by motorbikes 60
Figure 4 Route map: Alexandre III Tunnel to Alma Tunnel...........................61
Figure 5 Route map: Place de la Concorde to Alexandre III Tunnel 64
Figure 6 Brian Anderson's diagram of Mercedes surrounded by motorbikes 70
Figure 7 Diagram of motorcyclist's post-crash gesture seen by Levistre.......95
Figure 8 Photo of Mercedes' passenger side post-crash 96
Figure 9 Photo of Mercedes' driver's side post-crash 97
Figure 10 *Evening Standard* Final Edition 1 September 1997.....................119
Figure 11 Andanson photo of Gilbert Bécaud in his living room 124
Figure 12 Close-up of Bécaud's TV set 31 August 1997 125

ALAN POWER EXPOSED

Bibliography

Books

Burrell, P., (2003), *A Royal Duty*, Australia: Penguin Books
Foreign & Commonwealth Office, (1998), *The Diplomatic Service List 1998*, London, Her Majesty's Stationery Office
Morgan, J., (2007), *Cover-Up of a Royal Murder: Hundreds of Errors in the Paget Report*, USA: Amazon
————, (2009), *Diana Inquest: The Untold Story*, USA, Amazon
————, (2009), *Diana Inquest: How & Why Did Diana Die?*, USA, Amazon
————, (2010), *Diana Inquest: The French Cover-Up*, UK, Lightning Source
————, Editor, (2010), *Diana Inquest: The Documents the Jury Never Saw*, UK, Lightning Source
————, (2011), *Diana Inquest: The British Cover-Up*, UK, Lightning Source
————, (2012), *Diana Inquest: Who Killed Princess Diana?*, Australia, Shining Bright Publishing
————, (2012), *Paris-London Connection: The Assassination of Princess Diana*, Australia, Shining Bright Publishing
————, (2013), *Diana Inquest: Corruption at Scotland Yard*, Australia, Shining Bright Publishing
Morton, A., (1997), *Diana: Her True Story – In Her Own Words*, Australia: Harper Collins
Rees-Jones, T., & Johnston, M. (2000). *The Bodyguard's Story: Diana, The Crash and the Sole Survivor.* New York, USA: Warner Books Inc.
Simmons, S., (2005), *Diana: The Last Word*, London, Orion Books
Tomlinson, R., (2001), *The Big Breach*, Edinburgh, Cutting Edge

Websites

Amazon UK — www.amazon.co.uk
BBC News — http://news.bbc.co.uk
British Monarchy — www.royal.gov.uk
CNN — http://edition.cnn.com
Diana Conspiracy — www.dianaconspiracy.com/index.html
Flame
www.fantompowa.net/Flame/diana_eyewitness.htm
John Morgan's Investigation
www.princessdianadeaththeevidence.weebly.com
Metropolitan Police Service — www.met.police.uk
MPS Paget Report
www.met.police.uk/news/operation_paget_report.htm
National Archives — http://yourarchives.nationalarchives.gov.uk
Official Inquest at National Archives
http://webarchive.nationalarchives.gov.uk/20090607230718/http:/ww
w.scottbaker-inquests.gov.uk/
Public Interest
www.public-interest.co.uk/diana/dianaewa.htm
Richard Tomlinson Affidavit:
http://www.conspiracyplanet.com/channel.cfm?channelid=41&content
id=88
Royal Albert Hall — www.royalalberthall.com
Wikipedia — http://en.wikipedia.org/wiki/

Newspapers & Periodicals

Belgium: Death of Astrid, *Time* magazine, 9 September 1935
Dovkants, Keith & Laville, Sandra, Di's Driver Was Drunk, *Evening Standard*, 1 September 1997
Glauber, Bill, Charles, Di Reach Royal Settlement, *The Baltimore Sun*, 13 July 1996
Italiano, Laura, Scotland Yard Investigates Diana Slay Plot as Forthcoming Book Details Royal Conspiracy, 18 August 2013
Lord Mishcon Obituary, *The Independent*, 1 February 2006

BIBLIOGRAPHY

Lyall, Sarah, Her Royal Common-ness, *The New York Times*, 14 July 1996

Witness Saw a Second Car Flee the Crash Site, *USA Today*, September 21 1997

Media Documentaries, Interviews and Transcripts

Geraldo At Large, Interview with Alan Power and Imogen Lloyd-Webber, Fox News, 24 August 2013

The Panorama Interview, BBC, 20 November 1995, www.bbc.co.uk/politics97/diana/panorama

Unlawful Killing, Documentary Film, Allied Stars and Associated Rediffusion Productions, 2011

Reference Works

Soanes, C., & Hawker, S., (2005), Editors, *Compact Oxford English Dictionary of Current English*, UK, Oxford University Press

ALAN POWER EXPOSED

Author Information

John Morgan was born in Rotorua, New Zealand in 1957, and has lived in Australia for the last 25 years. He and his wife currently reside in Redcliffe, on the shores of Moreton Bay, near Brisbane.

John is an investigative writer with a diploma in journalism from the Australian College of Journalism. He completed his first book titled *Flying Free* in 2005 – about life inside a fundamentalist cult. Information regarding that book can be viewed at: www.flyingfree.zoomshare.com

In his earlier life John was an accountant for various organisations in Auckland and Sydney. Later during the 1990s, he became a retailer operating a shop on Sydney's northern beaches. Since the 1980s John travelled widely throughout the Pacific, Asia and the Middle East.

He retired in 2003 at the age of 46, after being diagnosed with a severe neurological illness called multiple system atrophy. After a year or two of coming to terms with that devastating turn of events, he eventually found that the forced retirement created an opportunity to fulfil a lifelong ambition to write.

Following the death of Diana, Princess of Wales in 1997, John developed an interest in the events that had led to the Paris crash. Since 2005 he carried out extensive full-time research into those events and studied the official British police report after it was published in late 2006. John subsequently completed a book on that subject in September 2007 – it was titled *Cover-Up of a Royal Murder: Hundreds of Errors in the Paget Report.*

Throughout 2008 John Morgan continued his investigations into the crash and closely followed the British inquest into the deaths of Princess Diana and Dodi Fayed. That research resulted in the initial volume of work on the inquest entitled *Diana Inquest: The Untold Story* – Part 1: *The Final Journey.* Six months later, during 2009, that

ALAN POWER EXPOSED

work was followed up with the second volume *Diana Inquest: How & Why Did Diana Die?* The third volume, entitled *Diana Inquest: The French Cover-Up* was published in 2010.

In 2009 John had received a large volume of unpublished documentation from within the official British police Paget investigation. As a result of that he was able – later in 2010 – to compile a dedicated volume entitled: *Diana Inquest: The Documents the Jury Never Saw*. That book was followed by Part 4, published in 2011, entitled *Diana Inquest: The British Cover-Up*.

During 2012 John's health continued to deteriorate, but he was still able to complete and publish two additional books – Part 5, *Diana Inquest: Who Killed Princess Diana?* and the page-turning summary of the shocking story, *Paris-London Connection: The Assassination of Princess Diana*.

Then in May 2013 John completed the sixth volume of the *Diana Inquest* series, *Corruption at Scotland Yard*.

John can be contacted at: shining.bright@optusnet.com.au

His investigation website is:

www.princessdianadeaththeevidence.weebly.com

Printed in Great Britain
by Amazon